A TO
OF COLWICK

Grenville Davies

Foreword By Stan Mellor M.B.E.

PRIDE OF PLACE PUBLISHING

PRIDE OF PLACE PUBLISHING LTD
PO BOX 70
CHORLEY
PR6 7SB

This Edition First Published in February 1994

ISBN 1-874645-03-5

Printed in Great Britain
by
Linotype, Blackburn.

This Book Is Dedicated To:-

My mother and father for planting the seed of interest. Tied Cottage for bringing that seed to life. Finally my wife and children for putting up with its continual growth over the last few years.

A TOUCH OF COLWICK
by G. Davies
Foreword by Stan Mellor, M.B.E.

**A Limited Edition of
1250 of which this is No. ...5.19...................**

Acknowledgements:-

First of all if I've forgotten to mention anyone my sincerest apologises. The list of people is endless, while their help has been overwhelming.

John Booth for taking the risk in publishing this book. Jeff Lord of Just-A-Sec in typing out the first chapter. Harry Holmes who for forty years did the building work at Colwick Park and has provided me with many a tale. Unfortunately a couple of them are not printable. The same can be said of Pat Deane and her late mother Mrs Phil Taylor, whose father worked for many years at Nottingham, the last thirty or so of them as head groundsman. Jan Entwhistle and Ann Whelbourne for letting me look through the files at Nottingham racecourse.

Special mention must be made of Chris Pitt, not least of all for suggesting the tongue in cheek title. I've lost count of the times I've phoned him up to check this date or that date in the form book. He has also done the job of proof reading. Someone else who has also done the job of leafing through the formbook for me is Stewart Nash. Leading racing writer Richard Onslow for his help and advice.

I would also like to thank Susan Woodward and Douglas Chrystall for converting my scrawl into Printed Text.

The staff at the Nottinghamshire Record Office. Also my colleagues at the Nottingham Local Studies Library especially

Dorothy Ritchie for devoting much of her spare time for going through the photos with me.

Bill Greenough of the Evening Post for his help in sorting out some photos.

Finally my sincerest thanks to Stan Mellor M.B.E. for agreeing to write the foreword.

Foreword

By Stan Mellor MBE.

Nottingham racecourse prompts numerous memorable occasions for me, both as a jockey and a trainer. I rode my first winner at the course in 1956 on a horse called Midox, for George Owen. Forty more were to follow, including a treble and eight doubles culminating in my one thousandth winner on Ouzo in 1971, a feat remembered with great relief as well as a tremendous thrill. Among Others I was delighted to ride a winner there for my childhood hero Tim Molony and I even rode two for Lord Lucan!

As a jockey, I regarded Nottingham as a fair track ,its long straight always giving horses a chance. As a trainer, I am honoured to have a race named after me, which I won with Moonstone Lad, on a day which completed a treble. Like many others I appreciate the course fences, which are fair and inviting for young chasers, making Nottingham a favourable track on which to run horses.

As recent facility improvements indicate, Nottingham Racecourse now has a forward looking, progressive management and I would like to take this opportunity to wish them good luck. I'm sure they will continue to give great pleasure to racegoers for years to come.

About The Author

Grenville Davies has been the secretary of the East Midlands Racing Club since 1989. He has a long standing love affair with his local track.He is also a committee member of the Federation of British Racing Clubs.

He has already contributed to a variety of racing magazines and written a brief history of Nottingham raccourse which was used in their racecards.

More recently in contributed to the book, Great Racing Gambles & Frauds Vol 3.

He works for Nottingam County Council Libraries and Lives in Nottingham with his wife and two children.

Contents

Select Chronology.

1689/1690

The Old Nottingham Racecourse opened.
Although no proper date can be ascertained it is generally
thought to be one of these two years.

30th July, 1761.

The Old Course saw a famous match between two great horses
of the time, Careless and Atlas

3rd July 1770.

The greatest horse and stallion of the 18th century , Eclipse won
the Kings Plate at Nottingham

1st February, 1777

The foundation stone for the grandstand was laid. A structure
that many other racecourses were to copy

3rd August 1779.

The Duke of Cumberland (Brother of George II) attended the
course to see his horse Pamona .

1831

There was no racing at Nottingham during this Year because of
threats made to injure horses by the Reform Rioters.

26th February 1867

Nottingham hosted its first races under National Hunt Rules.

2nd February, 1874

A racing dynasty was founded at Nottingham, As Mr J Ford became the first in a long line of the Ford family to be associated with the running of the track.

30 September 1890.

The old Nottingham racecourse on the Forest Recreation Ground closed down after a 200 year history.

19th August 1892

The present Nottingham racecourse at Colwick Park opened.

26 January 1931.

Golden Miller the greatest steeplechaser to grace the turf until the advent of Arkle, won at Nottingham.

3 October 1933.

Gordon Richard's (later Sir) rode the first of his world record 12 consecutive winners at Nottingham. The remaining eleven being at Chepstow on the 4th and 5th October.

26 March 1935.

 The Wragg brothers Arthur, Sam and Harry scored a 1-2-3.

2 November 1940.

The Cambridgeshire, Jockey Club Cup, Cheveley Park and Middle Park Stakes were held at Nottingham for the only time in the races history.

14 April 1941.

The Easter Monday Meeting crowd of over 41,000 people created a record attendance.

16 January 1958.

Two R.A.F. planes crashed above Colwick, the fuselage of one landing on the racecourse.

8 December 1959.

The race course station closed down.

1 May 1961.

The legal opening of betting shops and the first featured race was one from Nottingham.

9 July 1965.

The Nottingham Racecourse Company sold the course and land to the Nottingham City Council.

8 November 1965.

The City Council decided to keep Colwick Park for horse racing.

2 February 1967.

Francis Ford retired as Clerk of the Course, so ending a long line of the Ford family at both of Nottingham's courses. His successor was none other than John Hughes.

18 December 1971.

Stan Mellor became the first National Hunt jockey to ride 1000 career wins. This he achieved at Nottingham on Ouzo.

1 April 1974.

The first ever race in Britain for men and women riders.

4 July 1981.

Paul Cook made racing history by riding three winners at three different courses, in one day. The third winner coming at Nottingham.

13 August 1984.

Fillies Triple-Crown winner Oh So Sharp registered her first success as a two-year-old.

30 October 1984.

The following seasons Derby winner Slip Anchor also secured his first win at Nottingham.

13 August 1985.

Popular northern based jockey Edward Hide rode his last British winner on Hi-Tech Leader.

29 October 1985.

The day to end all days, for Lester Piggott 'retired' from race-riding. His last British winner coming on Full Choke, while his final ride was on Wind From The West.

23 March 1986.

A fire completely gutted the Tattersalls grandstand.

20 April 1987.

Former leading jockey Jonjo O'Neill opened the new Tattersalls grandstand.

23 September 1991.

Champion jockeys Steve Cauthen and Peter Scudamore lowered a time capsule into the ground in front of the members stand / weighing room complex.

15 February 1992.

Desert Orchid opened the new members stand / weighing room complex. The day was completed by the future champion hurdler Royal Gait winning.

Chapter One
A Four Mile Track

Even Nottingham's most famous sporting legend Brian Clough probably doesn't know everything, I am sure he his blissfully unaware that racing pre-dates football in the city by 200 years. Whilst the course at Colwick Park celebrated its centenary in 1992, racing had taken place on the Forest Recreation ground 200 years prior to that.

An Old Print Of The Forest Racecourse

Whilst the exploits of Brian Clough and his teams have grabbed most of the local back page sporting headlines, the racecourse has itself witnessed headline grabbing events in recent times 'Lester Piggott's retirement', and the disastrous fire of 1986 have seen to that. Brian Clough's reign may be at an end, but the racecourse goes from strength to strength and lets hope it goes on for another hundred years producing racing headlines.

Records conflict as to when the inaugural meeting was on the old course, but it is thought to be in 1689/1690 From the Corporation records for 1689 is the following:- *'The Hall (being the town council) at the request of the county gentlemen, resolved to subscribe towards a piece of plate to be run for at the races'.*

The track was originally four miles round and encompassed the areas of Basford, Forest Fields, Hyson Green, Lenton and Radford. Incidentally it also went under the name of Basford Lings. In 1751 Deering, in his History Of Nottingham, described the course thus:- *As a place of amusement in the racing line, there are but a few which are considered in any light competition with it. It has enough of variety for a rider to show his skill in the management of his racer, either on trying, easing or accommodating ground. Its turf is admirably calculated for sporting, here a gentle swell of the earth, there a gentle declivity?* He went on to state that *'Nottingham is one of the twelve towns where the King's Guineas (plates) are run for, besides other money plates. These races are kept in July, the course which formerly was four miles round, is at the time but two miles. It is one of the best in England, and is never out of order for running, be the weather what it will. Here is a fine valley for coaches, chariots to pass and reaps, and for the accommodation of the nobility and gentry, who come to the races. The Nottingham course could once have vied with any course in the Kingdom for a grand appearance of nobility, neither Newmarket nor Banstead Downs boast of a better company nor horses, but since the great increase of horse races it has rather dwindled. However the late Act Of Parliament has been of some service to it, and there seems a great likelihood that in a number of years it may recover its former lustre'.*

The act referred to, which was passed in 1740, raised the level of stakes to a minimum of £50, there being two exceptions to this, being Newmarket and Hambleton in North Yorkshire. There was a £200 fine for breaking the law.

At about this time Daniel Defoe (of Robinson Crusoe fame) travelled Britain, and the following extract is taken from his tour of Great Britain and Ireland Volume 2

'But the illustrious company at the Nottingham races was, in my opinion, the glory of the day; for there we saw, besides eleven or twelve noblemen, an infinitive throng of gentlemen from all the countries round nay, even out of Scotland it self, the appearance, in my opinion, greater, as it was really more numerous, than I ever saw at Newmarket, except when the king have been there in ceremony; for I cannot but say, that in the time of King Charles II, when his majesty used to be frequently at Newmarket, I have known the assembly there have been with far less company than this at Nottingham meetings, when the Mareschal Duke de Tallard was there, I should say, that no occasions at Newmarket, in my

memory, ever came up to it, except the first time that King William was there after the Peace of Ryswick.'

An added bonus for racegoers was a line of about twelve windmills that ran along Forest Road, which must have provided a magnificent backdrop to the course.

Although not everyone was a fan of the races, as can be evidenced by William Hutton, who wrote in his autobiography about this time in Nottingham during 1741, 'The week of the races is an idle one among the stockings at Nottingham. It was so with me. Five days had passed and I had done little more than the work of four.' At the time he was an apprentice in the hosiery industry.

The reduction in the length of the course to two miles took place in the early 18th century. In 1797 further alterations were made. This came about because the part of the forest that adjoined Lenton and Radford was enclosed. The following year a new course was laid out in the shape of a figure 8, but this received a definite thumbs down from the public as they couldn't see any racing, so in 1813 it was altered to an oval, of a mile and a quarter. A few alterations were later made, and in the middle of the 19th century, it was even claimed to be 'one of the most commodious and complete courses, both for horses and spectators, in the kingdom".'

There was no permanent grandstand until 1777 but it was well worth the wait, as the architect was John Carr who happened to be the leading designer of the time. The decision to build at Nottingham was taken at a meeting on 21st October 1776 at the

White Lion Inn in the town. A subscription list was started, the terms being that no one was allowed to subscribe less than twenty guinea's, which entitled the subscriber to two silver tickets, to be transferable. Each ticket admitted a lady or a gentleman during the races. A full list of the subscribers is reproduced below:-

Duke of Newcastle	200	gns.
Mr Jonathon Truman	20	gns.
Duke of Norfolk	300	gns.
Mrs Colin Elton	20	gns.
Duke of Portland	200	gns.
Mr Brand	20	gns.
Earl of Lincoln	200	gns.
Mr James Foxcroft	20	gns.
Earl of Stamford	50	gns.
Mr George Moody Brentall	20	gns.
Lord George Cavendish	30	gns.
Mt Thomas Hunt	20	gns.
Lord Edward Bentinck	200	gns.
Mr S Turner	20	gns.
Lord Middleton	100	gns.
J Newton, Esq	20	gns.
Lord Melbourn	50	gns.
W Emmerson, Esq	20	gns.
Sir Gervas Clifton	60	gns.
W.C. Sherbrooke, Esq	20	gns.
Sir George Saville	100	gns.
Job Charlton, Esq	20	gns.
Sir Charles Sedley	100	gns.
John Hewitt, Esq	50	gns.
Sir William Boothby	20	gns.
Rev. C. Launder	20	gns.
Sir Francis Molyneux	20	gns.
Mrs Jerom	20	gns.

John Musters Esq	100	gns.
Mr Alderman Carruthers	20	gns.
E.T. Gould, Esq	20	gns.
Mr Thomas Rawson	20	gns.
Anthony Ayre, Esq	50	gns.
Mr H Parker	20	gns.
John Sherwin Esq	20	gns.
Sir Thomas Parkyns, Bart	20	gns.
Abal Smith	50	gns.
John Kirk, Esq.	20	gns.
Cornelius Launder, Esq.	20	gns.
Rev. Mr. Nixon	20	gns.
John Westcomb Emerton, Esq	20	gns.
Mr John Foxcroft	20	gns.
John Whetham, Esq	20	gns.
John and Thomas Wright	40	gns.
Dr. White	20	gns.
Mr Samuel Statham	20	gns.
Mr Richard Dodson	20	gns.
Mr Thomas Martion	20	gns.

Subsequently Nottingham Corporation granted a lease of the ground to a group of Lords and Gentlemen, led by Lord Edward Bentinck. The lease though contained a covenant that in the event of a Town Enclosure Act, such a leasehold property should immediately revert to the corporation; this eventually happened in 1845.

The foundation stone of the grandstand was laid on February 1st 1777. It was a magnificent structure, The lower storey was occupied by tea and card rooms, while the upper floor was set aside for entertainments. The lead covered roof offered standing room for 500 patrons and apparently it was packed to the rafters at every meeting. The 81ft. stand is no longer there as the remnants were eventually pulled down in 1912. To the south of the track it was sloped which provided a natural amphitheatre for spectators, which happened to be free. Admission was only charged for entrance to the Grandstand and Silver Ring enclosures.

Of all the races the old course saw, the one that caused most interest occured in 1761 and was between Careless owned by Mr John Borlace and the Duke of Devonshire's Atlas. The two protagonists had already met at York on 30th August 1760, when Atlas was the victor, but not everyone was satisfied by the result, and arguments raged as the regards the merits of the two horses, so a rematch was arranged. The general belief was that Careless would prove superior and Nottingham, virtually to a man, 'put their money where their mouth's were. Despite weight of money behind Careless, Atlas confirmed his supremity.

But even that race paled in comparison to a race held there on 21st April 1773, for as the Nottingham Date Book records:

'The Journal states that upwards of fifteen thousand people assembled this day on the Nottingham Race Course to witness a foot race between two of the most noted pedestrians of the day, Harrison of Staffordshire, and Granny of Belper. The spectators were from all parts of the country, and the greatest possible interest was felt in the issue. The friend of the Derbyshire runner were so enthusiastic in their support of his pretensions, that many of them sold their beds, cows, and swine, to raise money to make bets; and others pawned their wives' wedding rings for that purpose; for as odds were seven to four and three to two in favour of Harrison, the temptation became

so much the stronger, and very considerable bets laid. The highest odds we hear of were one hundred pounds, laid by a gentleman in the stand, to thirty. The match was for the sum of £200, and the distance ten miles, or five times round the course (it being then two miles in extent). At two o'clock the competitors stripped, and when entirely naked, for they ran without any covering whatever, instantly commenced their arduous struggle. For the first seven miles the contest was well sustained, but in running the fourth time round, Granny by some accident fell lame on his right leg, and Harrison gained nearly fifty yards on him, which Granny could not with his utmost efforts recover, but rather kept losing ground, though in running the tenth mile he made one grand push to recover it in coming down the hill, but very nearly falling in the attempt; his courage and strength then failing, he gave up the contest, with tears flowing from his eyes. The race was performed in exactly fifty-six minutes and two seconds.'

Chapter Two
Georgian And Victorian

Like most courses at this time cock fighting and horse racing were promoted jointly and indeed in many cases the racing was just a mere side show. For most of the 18th century it was the done thing to wind up the races with a main event of cock fighting.

Nottingham Races From A Painting By John Holland c1860. There Is A Large Degree Of Artistic Licence As The Stand Has One Tier Too Many.

For the period 1777-79 the course was at the height of its popularity. August 3rd 1779 saw a royal visit by the Duke of

Cumberland, brother to George II, who was subsequently given the freedom of the town. The Duke was in attendance to see his horse Pamona run, but it went down to the 7-4 favourite, Honest Robin, in the Nottingham Sweepstakes. Of the eleven runners, seven were by the great sire, Herod. It was also an indictment of the time that four of the runners were unnamed. The race card was headed by a woodcut which showed horses galloping over the Lings, spectators in a grandstand, while a gentleman is weighing in at the starting post. The card ends with 'The old song of Moor's Ramble to Nottingham horse races'. It shows that the entries were incomplete, the verses probably being added after the races were over:-

I'll tell thee Dick where I've lately been,
O rare Nottingham Town,
I put up my horse at the White Lion Inn,
O rare Nottingham Town,
And there were rich doings as ever were seen,
O rare Nottingham Town,
When I saw their large vaults down i' th' rock deep and fine,
O rare Nottingham Town,
So plenteously stored with strong ale and rich wine,
O rare Nottingham Town,
Thought I to myself, Oh were this but all mine,
O rare Nottingham Town.

The ballad goes on to tell of the first heat:-
Two horses not tinee foot asunder came in,
And a third with his nose about halfway between.

Around this time the race week was completed by a grand ball at the Assembly Rooms, in the city; But towards the end of the 18th century racing appears to have hit a significant bad patch in terms of quantity of runners. This was probably due to the loss of two local turf parsons, Sir Charles Sedley and Mr John Borlas Warren. In August 1795 the entries became so bad that on the first day, the King's Plate, worth 100 guinea's, was walked over by Mr Hutchinson's Constitution. On the third day as described in the Racing Calendar the meeting had to be abandoned ' for want of horses.'

The Forest also provided the setting for a wedding reception as the following extract taken from Victorian Nottingham Volume 10 (1973) by Richard Iliffe and William Baguley, published by the Nottingham Historical Film Unit, describes,

" In the summer of 1801 four Nottingham butchers were married on the same day, and with their friends, held a jovial wedding picnic in the shade of the Grandstand. The proceedings commenced with a foursome donkey race, each bridegroom mounting a 'Neddy' to cover half the racecourse, the winner to receive the expenses of his wedding day from the other three victims.The four benign looking steeds were bedecked with mascots from the wardrobes of the ladies. One animal was neckerchiefed with a pair of long stockings; another had a pair of stays attached to his tail with a bow of green ribbon; the third was saddled with a night-gown; and the fourth wore a voluminous pair of ladies 'nether garments'. Needless to say, this animal finished last; the one adorned with the stays proved an easy winner. "

The year 1831 was very much a non-event as there was no racing at all on the course. This was the period in British history when the Reform Riots were sweeping the country. In fact it was the nearest to revolution that Britain has ever been. After persistent threats to injure horses racing at Nottingham, the meeting was cancelled.

NOTTINGHAM RACES.

No Person will be allowed to place or have any Booth, Shew, Carriage, Stall, Barrow, Hamper, or other Article on any part of the Nottingham Forest during the ensuing Races, without the previous leave of the Race Committee, or the Corporation Collectors.

No Ale or Spirits will be permitted to be placed for Sale on any part of the ground in front of the Booths; nor will any Stall or Barrow be allowed except on the ground appointed by the Collectors.

All Payments must be made in advance, and those for the Booths and other erections will be called for on MONDAY AFTERNOON, JULY 19th instant, on the ground.

Any Party not conforming to this Notice, will be immediately discharged, and not allowed to place any Booth, Stall, or other Article at any future Races.

Proper Persons will be appointed to see these regulations carried out.

By Order of the Committee,

WM. ENFIELD, Town Clerk.

July 15th, 1847.

R. ALLEN, PRINTER, NOTTINGHAM

A Scarce Surviving Racecourse Notice From 1847

Many famous horses have appeared on the old course, and without a shadow of a doubt, the most influential to appear was Eclipse. Over 90% of thoroughbreds racing today can trace one line (or more) back to Eclipse. He was never extended in 18 races, and he had a walkover at Nottingham in the July 3rd, 1770 King's Plate. (All opponents were scratched)

Eclipse: (From The Famous Sartorius Oil Painting) Had A Walkover At Nottingham In 1770.

1836 saw the appearance of the previous years Derby winner Mundig in the King's Plate, a race he won with comparative ease.

But the most remarkable horse, if not the toughest to run at the old course, was the 1858 Ascot Gold Cup Winner, Fisherman. He won Nottingham's Trial Stakes at the 1856 Spring Meeting. He followed up with further victories there in each of the next three seasons. Fisherman had a total of 70 wins from 121 starts, including a season record of 23 victories which he achieved in 1856. The horse was later exported to Australia and became a very influential sire.

A great race mare always seems to have a certain aura about her, and certainly one of the most popular was Alice Hawthorn. She turned out in October 1843 beating King of Trumps, without trouble in both heats. Her roll of honour includes the 1842 Chester Cup, and the 1843 and 1844 Doncaster Cups. Generally speaking a race mare of any note turns out to be a very poor breeder. That did not apply in this case as she went on to foal the 1860 Derby winner Thormanby.

Of the many Derby winners that have run at Nottingham one of the most interesting was St Gatien who won a small two year old race in 1843. He then went on to dead heat in the Derby with Harvester. Yet neither horse can be said to have been champion of their generation. Another three year old that year was St Simon arguably one of the greatest horses of all time. Fortunately for the connections of St Gatien and Harvester, St Simon was only entered for one classic, the 2,000 Guineas; but even then that entry was declared void, when his owner, Prince Batthany dropped dead at Newmarket at the end of the horse's two year old season. Of particular local interest is that St Simon was subsequently bought by the Duke of Portland, who later stood him at Welbeck Estate near Worksop, North Nottinghamshire, where he was to found a racing dynasty.

As mentioned earlier, 1845 saw the Town Enclosure Act, so under the terms of the lease, the Nottingham Corporation immediately took charge of the course. Mr W Page was elected as Race Committee Chairman, while Mr J G Birley of Doncaster was appointed Clerk of the Course, A post previously held by Mr W Lacey. The following year the meeting was transferred back to August, for the first time since 1835.

The following are extracts from the diary of Samuel Collinson, a stockbroker who came to Nottingham in 1845 from Hull; he was the dramatic and fine art critic for the Nottingham Journal, and also an artist and poet.

I make no apologies for including this quote in its entirety as its contemporary observations give a superb insight into 19th Century racing.

<u>Wed. August 5th 1846.</u>
First Race Day. My dear wife accompanied me to the racecourse. The weather glorious - the hill side covered with merry makers enjoying themselves, some under cover of the booths, others with better taste preferred to sun themselves in the open air and breathe the invigorating breeze. On the low ground amongst the carriages, from any indications that the deportment of the people offered, a spectator might just as easily have judged that the crowd was collected to attend a political meeting, as a mere holiday or recreation - so much quiet gravity, almost solemnity, pervades the middle and upper classes of this country. On the hillside amongst

the humbler classes, you would find more of what would remind you of what you had been accustomed to consider as Merrie England. Good humoured groups sat on the green turf, joking and passing round mugs of Nottingham Ale. They looked as happy as if they never had been and never would be, shut up from early morn to dewy eve, in close factories or closer attics, barely able by long hours and hard work to earn enough to sustain existence.

June 15 1856.

First Race Day. Fine morning. Afternoon to the races, great number of people present. I think more blacklegs than I ever noticed there, a more villainous looking lot it is scarcely possible to conceive. At night fireworks in the Arboretum, not very good, and not many persons present as I expected.

Friday 20th Feb. 1857.

Dull mild day. Went up to the top of Mansfield Road, looked in the Church Cemetery. Then to view Moses Wood's latest absurdity in the Architectural line. This is a lodge for the keeper of the ground about the Racecourse. It is a cruciform Grecian Temple built of brick, and it will be all columns and stucco. The Town Council ought to be ashamed of spending the towns money in such a manner.

Wed 22nd July 1857.

Light showers alternating with sunshine. Afternoon to the races, very fine crowd of people there. I saw some curious scenes, men well known, occupying respectable positions, aye, married men, sitting in the drinking places at the stand with an assemblage of whores, standing treat and hail fellow well met.

Tues. March 9th 1858.

All covered with snow and frost very keen. Snow falling at intervals all forenoon. Dirty sloppy day. Afternoon to Simpsons along with Chapman. Afterwards up to the Church Cemetery with him. Great excavations going on there, in connection with the works on the Forest now being carried out by the unemployed poor. The Forest is a Bitterly cold place to be at work upon such a day as this. The wind comes sweeping in from the N.W. blowing the sand and gravel in your face as sharp as pin points.

Shrove Tuesday Mar 8th 1859.

Alternate sunshine and cloud. A few drops of rain about 10am, a few snowflakes fall and then bright sunshine. One o' clock hailing. 1.5 sunshining. 2 snowing fast. About 3 o'clock in bright sunshine I walked to the racecourse. The horses were being started for the Notts. Stakes; upwards of an hour elapsed before a fair start could be made. Then came on a squall, and snow, then sunshine, then another race, after which it began to snow heavily and I came home.'

In 1847 the Nottingham Handicap was inaugurated. One of the leading races of the day, the purse was regularly in excess of £600. Among its early winners were Inheritress who also won the Queen's Plate two years in succession, Maid of Masham, Typee, Pretty Boy, Newcastle, Wallace and Atherstone. Pretty Boy's victory came between his success's in the Liverpool Cup and Goodwood Stakes.

The year 1853 saw a major move for the course, as it managed to gain two meetings. Apart from the August meet there was a Spring one (if you could call it that) as it was on the

8th February. A successful one it was too, the main race was the Nottingham Spring Handicap of 10 sovereigns each, with 50 added. The others being a sweepstake of 5 sovereigns each, with 25 sovereigns and 30 sovereigns added; a hurdle race of 5 sovereigns with 40 added; and a Hunter Stakes of 2 sovereigns with a Silver Cup.

An Early Racecard

The star local jockey of the period was John 'Brusher' Wells, champion jockey in 1853 and 1854. His double at the meeting on Duet in the Bunney Park two-year-olds Stakes and Le Julf in the Portland Handicap was a minor contribution to the Warwickshire-born rider's total of wins amassed on the Midlands tracks. Wells was noted for his eccentricity of dress, and thought nothing of riding work in a feathered Alpine hat, Gordon tartan suit and red Morocco slippers, but as Sir Joseph Hawley, for whom Wells rode five classic winners including three Derbies, remarked: 'I don't care how he dresses, he is a good enough jockey for me.'

John Wells: Local Hero And Twice Champion Jockey

At the 1867 spring meeting which was on the 26th and 27th of February, the stewards in attendance included the Duke of Hamilton, the Marquis of Hastings and his arch enemy in love Mr Henry Chaplin.

They fell out over the affections of a certain Lady Florence Paget. Miss Paget left Mr Chaplin vertually standing at the alter to elope with the Marquis. The Marquis was later financially ruined over his laying against Mr Chaplins horse Hermit in the Epsom Derby that year. The Marquis ended his days destitute when he died a year later aged 26 and the last words he spoke were 'Hermits Derby broke my heart. But I didn't show it, did I?' His widow later married Sir George Chetwymd(Whom we Shall hear of later).

The Duke of Hamilton won the days big race (25th February) the one and 1/4 miles Nottingham Spring Handicap with Beadle, ridden by A. Edwards. Although he must have appreciated this victory it is reasonable to assume that his attentions were focused elsewhere for the Duke also owned that years Grand National winner Cortolvin which won the following day.

On the second day of the meeting Nottingham held its first race under National Hunt Rules, when Mr C. Fletton's Orne won the Great Annual Hurdle over 2½ miles. His winning jockey Mr W. White later in the afternoon completed a double for he won The Hunt Cup, which was a Hurdle race for Hunters. The race going to Verdi which was owned by a Mr T. Wilkinson. Although National Hunt races took place at the Spring Meeting of the 1870's and were popular with the paying public. They never aspired to any great heights.

On July 19th 1867, the Nottingham Review gave a report of the Nottingham meeting which took place eight days earlier in which its said 'Nottingham has always been classed as one of the finest and cleanest places in the midland counties, and the course , which has undergone endless repairs of late, and which is now considered one of the best in England, is quite an ornament to our Ancient town, and may it keep so for generations to come. There have been several improvements made within the betting enclosure since the last meeting, a new wing having been added to the Grand Stand near to Hyson Green - Road, for the accommodation of betting gentleman who have hitherto found great inconvenience on the stand from there not being sufficient standing room. The ring, which was formerly considered too small has also been enlarged, it being extended to the side of the race-course, and now Palifadef enclosing it - a desideratum which has long been required. On the forest we noticed several shows, roundabout et c., which seems to be doing a thriving business, and amongst other games was the 'Californian Put' (A swindling transaction with three cards), and how anybody could stand and squander pounds upon pounsds it is really astonishing. The stand and the betting enclosure were well patronised by the sporting fraternity, and amongst the aristocracy where Lord Westmorland, Lord Bateman, Marquis of Hastings, Duke of St Albans, and Col. Forester; and on the balcony could be obeserved the Marchioness of Hastings. (aforementioned Florence Paget) and other distinguised ladies.'

Chapter Three
The Beginning of the Ford Era!

1869 saw a great deal of criticism levelled not so much at the course, but more at the ones who provided the raw material - the owners and trainers. As one local writer put it, " *With such an excellent course, magnificent enclosure, and capital ground for witnessing the races, the fields should be so small and the class of horses engaged so moderate.*" This particular year also happened to see the inaugural running of the Biennial Stakes of 10 sovereigns each with 100 sovereigns added for two-year-olds. It was won by Agility, a full sister to Apology, the winner of the 1874 St. Leger. Both horses were owned by Parson King, however this is not the name you will see in the record books, as he raced under the name of Mr Launde. The reason being he did not wish to offend his Bishop. Unfortunately not every follower of the Lord had such sincere thoughts towards horse racing as the genial parson. The main route to the course from the city centre was via Goldsmith and Waverley, and in the mid 19th Century there was a sign printed on a house wall in Goldsmith Street which showed a finger pointing and said: "To the Races. The Way to Hell". Quite what effect this had on racegoers is hard to say.
By the 1870's the racecourse was facing problems from fairground rides as the Race Committee Minute Book No 1 tells.

<u>13th April 1878   Meeting Race Committee</u>

Resolved that orders be given to the policemen at the several lodges to fasten gates at each entrance the night before the races so as to prevent roundabouts from being taken onto the forest.

September 1882 Illegal Betting

Resolved that notices be posted in the enclosures and the stand, cautioning persons against illegal betting at the ensuing meeting.

One of the most popular owners of the late 19th Century at Nottingham was Mr Henry Savile of Rufford Abbey. His best win was the 1872 Queen's Plate with Uhlan who prevailed after a titanic duel with the red hot favourite Agility.

Another close finish was witnessed for the 1874 Midsummer Handicap, which involved Mr Vyner's Thunder.The mount of Jim Gouter, in opposition, just happened to be the foremost rider of the time, Fred Archer.Thunder though carrying 8st 10lb managed to prevail by a neck. The excitement generated by his victory was so intense, that even those who had laid against him joined in the shouting. All distances from six furlongs to two miles came alike to him. The following season he was to win Epsom's City and Suburban Handicap under 9st 4lb in a common canter. Apart from being tough the horses seemed to have been a lot more versatile in those days.

Also in 1874, Mr. W.J.Ford took over as Clerk of the Course, and so began a long line of Fords to hold the post of Clerk of the Course at Nottingham. Other courses they officiated at include the long defunct Birmingham and Derby, plus one in North Nottinghamshire, Retford Hunt. With his appointment the quality of the racing at Nottingham improved; and by 1879 Spring Handicap was worth nearly 500 sovereigns.

As in common with most racecourses at the time, Nottingham suffered from some of the less desirable elements of society. So as the local magazine Jackdaw reported in 1879:

' *Nottingham Races produced the usual crop of Police Court Cases. An excursionist missed his train, and trying to travel by an ordinary, was fined accordingly. Arthur Slim had to pay the stout sum of 26s. for refusing to pay a cab fare. Nellie Madin, William Whittle, John Knight, and W. Clayton were fined for being drunk. It cost William Smith 30s. for selling fruit on the racecourse with unjust scales and light weights. George Walker, a cabman, got into controversy with his fare and endeavoured to drive him into the country instead of to the Police Station, for which eccentricity the magisterial charge was 40s. John Lorenz got drunk and was 'quodded' by a cabman for not paying him, which the bench deemed was worth 15s. Frank Snowden got three months for pocket pinching. The Jackdaw fails to contain the records of "respectable drunks", domestic dissenions, tattered garments, painted eyes, empty purses and bilious headaches which afflicted the "just", and opened the Easter holidays.*

Sam Jackson, a coloured man, has to pick oakum for two months, for breaking two panes of glass because they would not let him play his old banjo in the vaults of the Victoria Hotel. Sam hoped his fate might have been different, could a witness have been brought from Narrow Marsh. All the description he could give of her was "that she's a lady who belongs to a gentleman that goes about the town and ties himself up with rope". With such a slim clue it is scarcely the fault of the police that the lady was not forthcoming. '

Later in the same year, the 'Jackdaw' of 3rd October contained a description of the autumn race meeting:

Those who have been to the seaside resorts or interior watering places of this tight little island are scarcely sorry at the advent of October, and the prospect of unmitigated labour for the winter months. Such regard the autumn fairs and races as a sort of last spree before the long farewell to outdoor pleasure, and they abandon themselves accordingly to the spirit of the hour. But to the humble majority of male and female workers there is scarcely any holiday looked forward to with the anxiety with which this autumn carnival is anticipated. They have slaved for it, and saved for it, for a month. If they had the chance, they worked for it night and day for a fortnight; putting in, as the Sheffielders say, first a "cow" week then a "bull" week, that they may free their best clothes from pledge and be generally able to furnish up their outsides and to have a bit in hand to spend on a pint or lay on a fancy. Not only is the town all alive for fun, but the neighbouring villages catch the contagion of excitement and seem to invade the big village bodily. The railways are preternaturally busy, and the stations are scenes of all confusion and discordance. Affectionate wives and mothers are always losing their husbands and their children, and sweethearts have old Harry's time of it keeping an eye on the fellows in the refreshment saloons. The railway officials are naturally aggravated that they are in the jovial crowds, yet not one of them, but confined to monotonous duty; and it is not to be wondered at if they take their revenge by running a few loitering sewlls off their feet by a luggage laden truck, to the delight of the loiterers who by good luck avoid collision.

This is Jehu's harvest time. Fares doubled, hansoms, cabs and brakes desperately cannon against each other, drivers shout and swear, and passengers are run in by sheer physical force. As for the tramcars, the holiday makers are packed inside like herrings, and hang outside wherever there is a foot of standing room, or an inch of footboard or railing to grasp. There is no pity then for the wretched horses who strain, sweat, blow, and suffer untold agonies as the merciless whip descends on their unfortunate hides. Policemen find it best to philosophical and stick their thumbs in their belts, unless something exceptionally awful ruffles the official calm and makes interference absolutely imperative. Vehicles fight along the carriageways with hairbreadth escapes, which make the hair of the Agents of the Accident Assurance Companies stand on end, especially when some aristocrat drag with a couple of tooting dashes into the melee as if prepared to ride over very obstruction, and the footpaths converging on the course are flooded with the heterogeneous human steam.

The young and the strong are pitiless to age and youth, and it seems miraculous that mothers manage to save their toddling children from being trodden underfoot. As we near the course, the enterprising vendors of the "Correct card" run races with the carriages, dash in and out among the pedestrians, and manage in the confusion by overcharging greenhorns, or disappearing without giving change, to double their legitimate profits. Whence have all the patterers, chanters and beggars come? Wherever they do exist in the meantime, the same specimens reappear at the races. Sailors without arms and legs bray out nautical songs, the cracked voices of men and women, with children in arms and at heel, croak pitifully of no work to do, or rasp out sanguinary recitals of horrid murders; while *"downy blokes" do a roaring trade in the old swindle of "gining away" sealed packets, falsely warranted to contain ten times value received in either money, jewellery or indecency.*

The same swings, roundabouts and shooting galleries, the same strength and lung testers, the same gingerbread, butterscotch, and fried fish stalls, and in fact, all the same sights and sounds of a year ago meet once more, those holiday makers desperately struggling to obtain a vantage point on the course.

See over there, a pretty pair of villains who have come over from London on a bit of business. Though the sharp eyes of the detectives are upon them, it will be advisable to look well after watches and purses in their immediate vicinity. Indeed, forewarned and forearmed, and visitors who do not keep tickets and coin well out of the reach of light fingers on suck occasions need not go weeping and complaining to the police if they allow themselves to be robbed. It is well not to be deceived by appearances either, for there are plenty of swell mobsmen, at the other end of the criminal scale to the short piped characters above, whose dress and jewellery are ostensibly unexceptionable and who are thus carefully got up to give them facilities for throwing the unwary off their guard, and preying upon them

But this is thirsty work. Let us to the bar of the Grandstand or one of those licenced tents. Jostling is the order of the day, and those who decline to jostle, or are too modest to shout, must be content not to drink . Certainly there is no undue facility for drinking afforded, and the man who gets refreshment for himself and his wife or sweetheart has had to earn it by a brave struggle with knees and elbows, through knots of boozers and nymphs of easy virtue. These are the fortunate accidents of all large gatherings.

Elsewhere on the stand and the course, however, there is plenty of easy room and respectable company with which the most punctilious need not be afraid or ashamed to mingle. We can see representatives of our "old nobility", of our great manufacturers, of our enterprising merchants, of our intelligent farmers, artisans and working men, in family groups of old and young, who have come out to gratify the thorough English love of the horse, by witnessing the contentions of those famous thoroughbreds whose owners are attracted to our Races by the excellent stakes which the promoters are now able to offer. To these groups, this is a most exhilarating holiday, whether they have backed their opinion or not; and from close observations we should say that at least three quarters of the vast assemblage are entirely of indulgence in betting. We hope the "ministers of religion", who from fear of contamination, are looking on at the greatest possible distance through telescopes, will note this gratifying fact. These people love the horse and the glorious thrill of the race, but have no share in the illegitimate excitement of gambling, which has become an excrescence on all sports, however proper and harmless in themselves. The minority we must admit, are breathlessly listening to the shouts of those satchelled gentlemen and their clerks, whose "six to four on the fee-yald!" and "Three to one bar one!" resound all over the grounds; and who are exchanging tickets for coin with all the rapidity of a check-taker at a theatre on a crowded night. The amount of business quietly transacted by this clean-shaven, corpulent old swell, in velteen coat and vest, white hat, "loud trousers" and heavy jewellery, who admittedly hails from the capital of brass and Brummagen, is simply immense. Such as these, however, and the more aristocratic swells within the enclosure, are the legitimate bankers of the "ring" who are safe to "pony up", if fortune should happen to favour the backer. This is more than can be said of these gentlemen who, like Joseph, wear coats of many colours, and parti-coloured hats Joseph's father never dreamed of. They are more or less "black sheep", and therefore graze on the edge of the course at a very respectable distance from the "bonton" of the betting fraternity. They can accommodate you with all sorts of adds and indulge you in all varieties of investments "run or not"; but if the favourites happen to win and you hear the cry of "welsher!" you will see one man running across the field, leaping fences and dodging the crowd as if a sleuthhound were at his heels; and another being knocked about by the crowd and his clothes torn to pieces, while a bobby looks smilingly on; you may then be sure that the "bank" of a couple of these varied gentlemen has been broken, and that the betters, whom they cannot pay, are taking their change out according to the most approved principles of "Turf Lynch Law".

What a supreme quarter of an hour is that after the "bell has rung for a race". The telegraph indicates the starters, and every man and woman has a choice, necks are craned towards the saddling paddock and the preliminary gallop is breathlessly watched; the voices of the bookmakers are as loud as the tongues of ancient Babel; a false start is made and then the half dozen horses get well away in a body; the spectators hold their breath and the stillness and silence are oppressive; the gay jackets of the jockeys round the corner with a flash like a rainbow; the winner is past the post and the crowd give tongue with a roar like the voice of many waters. The disappointment of the losers is lost sight of in the ecstasy of the *winners. Here, just behind us, is a young lady who cannot have done more than win a pair of gloves, and yet she waves her handkerchief, dances with glee, and almost embraces us in the exuberance of her triumph.*

One advantage of races and outdoor sports is the long interval between drinks, caused by the interest in each event; and if the same crowd were gathered together without racing or running to claim the bulk of their attention, the result would be deplorable.

It was very ungallant, nevertheless, of many lovers, husbands or fathers, to get so engrossed in speculation as to leave their wives and sweethearts to take care of themselves for a considerable time. We felt a really tender pity for one lady who was left for hours together like a wallflower, and in whose blue eyes the tears shone when the recent Knight at last came up to make his peace with lying lips.

Yes Reverend sir, there were a few robberies, a few drunks, a few fights, but we beg you to say not an iota more than a similar crowd must inevitably produce until you manage to wash human nature more effectively than you yet appear able to do. We have no hesitation in saying that the Autumn Races produced an amount of happy exhilaration among the great majority of the pleasure seekers, which amply justifies their continued existence,'

As a postscript to the above, the following item appeared in the 'Jackdaw' a week later, on 19th October 1879:

In the 1870's a tower was built at the top of Waverly Street, by a Mr Hammersley to enable him to watch racing on the Forest from the comfort of his home. It is one hundred and twelve steps to the top.

' A notice appeared in the window of the Nottingham University Building, prohibiting the male members of the staff from attending the horse races under the pain of instant dismissal. Apparently one highly positioned member of the Faculty, instead of staying by the notice to see it complied with, "was to be seen on the course at three p.m., card and pencil in hand, with a look on his face that boded ruin for all the bookmakers through the desperate investment of his solitary shilling".'

Owners of the calibre of the Duke of St Albans, Sir John Astley, Sir George Chetwynd and Captain Machell, used to regularly enter their horses at Nottingham.

Sir John Astley, known to one and all as "The Mate", owned Peter the Royal Hunt Cup and Hardwicke Stakes winner at Royal Ascot of 1881. A prodigious gambler on his own horses, and while he never made a great deal of money he was no fool, and was straight and honest as the day is long. He was a one time M.P. for North Lincolnshire, and whilst at a political meeting, he was asked as to what did he think of Sir Wilfred Lawson's Liquor Bill, *but I know that mine is a duced sight too high this year".*

It would be harder to find anyone other than Captain Machell who has been associated with so many top class horses, both national hunt and flat, during the last century. Horses that he either owned, trained or managed include: Grand National winners Disturbance 1873, Reugny 1874, Regal 1876 and Seaman 1882; Derby winners Hermit 1876 and Harvester 1884. But his best horse, indeed one of the top half a dozen horses of the 1800's was the 1893 Triple Crown winner Isinglass. With some shrewd and calculated betting he was able to buy back the family estate at Westmorland. As a party trick he'd the ability to do a standing jump onto a mantle piece.

Like the previous two, Sir George Chetwynd was very knowledgeable about his racing, but he had no scruples. Indeed he was involved in one of the famous libel cases of the 19th Century. It centred around Lord Durham's speech at the 1887 Gimcrack Dinner at York where he called into question the running of Chetwynd' s horses. Chetwynd claimed £20,000 damages, and eventually, near on two years later, the case came to court. Although he won, he was awarded a derisory farthing, the ultimate insult. Sir George Chetwynd immediately resigned from the Jockey Club and the Turf.

An Early Postcard With The Forest Stand In The Background

But the most formidable owner of the late 19th Century was Mr Manton, to give her proper title, the Duchess of Montrose, or as people often used to call her, "Carrie Red". Generally speaking she had a heart of gold, but if you got the wrong side of her, she would cut you down with one lash of her sharp, vindictive tongue. At the October meeting of 1884 her best horse Thebais (who won the 1881 1000 Guineas and Oaks) won the Queen's Plate by a neck from the Doncaster Cup hero Louis d'or. Incidentally this was the last occasion on which a Queen's Plate was raced for at Nottingham. As regards the King's / Queen's Plates, they originated in the reign of Queen Anne, and were provided by the privy purse until their abolition in 1887.

Thebais's jockey was Fred Archer," The tinman" - a very close friend of "Carrie Red", and many folk say even closer. However reproduced below from Also Ran by Billy Brown, published by E Hulton & Co., in 1923, is a story concerning "The Tinman which to say the least, will make your eyes water. Billy Brown had over 50 years experience in racing as a stable lad, jockey, trainer and owner.

" I ran a mare of mine named Calabria in a race at Nottingham (old course) on April 9th 1879. She appeared to be winning easily 100 yards from the Judges Box and 10-1 was shouted on her doing so, but suddenly she stopped as though she had broken one of her hind legs, and Archer's mount won by a length. I ran down to meet her and ascertain the cause of her sudden stop.

Barlow, her jockey, said she must have put her hind leg in a hole. I went round to see if I could find anything on the offside of the mare, and lo and behold, blood was streaming down the offside of her hind leg, wherein a good-sized gash had been made by a spur.

Fred Archer: Rode Dual Classic Winner Thebais To Win The Queens Plate In October 1884

No wonder the mare stopped as suddenly as she did. Master Fred had put his long leg out and spurred the mare in a tender place. No doubt he had been annoyed by Barlow trying to beat him on the post by a head or a neck, instead of going on and winning as he did by several lengths."

This incident evidently shows two things about Fred Archer's character, his never say die attitude and his often callous, brutal treatment of horses, particularly in his early years. By the way, he got the nickname "The Tinman" over his love of money , as Tin was Victorian slang for money.

In its last few years the biggest problem that seemed to concern the race committee was the toilet facilities for the patrons, due to complaints from the Noel Street residents (on the west side of the track), as these Race Committee Minutes prove.

24th. December 1886. Temporary Urinal at Races.

Resolved that better urinal accommodation be provided near the Refreshment Booths so as to prevent the nuisance and annoyance complained of by the residents of houses in Noel Street and that the chairman be authorised to have such arrangements made as he may consider necessary .

14th. Feb. 1887. Urinal Accommodation at Races.

Resolved that a canvas screen be erected at the rear of the Refreshment Booths to prevent persons using the temporary urinal from being seen from Noel Street and that Mr Metcalf be employed to put up the same.

The October meeting of 1884 saw an oddity for the first time in over 13 years on any British racecourse. The oddity in question was a double dead-heat. Eventually they decided to split the spoils of the Friar Tuck Selling Plate between Scotch Pearl and Candahar II. The big race of the meet was the Nottingham Handicap worth over £500 which went to Antler, who defeated the previous year's 1,000 Guineas winner Hauteur.

The gulf that existed between National Hunt and Flat racing was never better illustrated that at the 1885 meeting, when Roquefort, that year's Grand National winner, was turned over by what was basically a selling plater, in a mile and a half flat race.

Racecourses nowadays still have the occasional problem from dogs, or rather the horses do. But this was nothing compared to the last century, when many a meeting was unenclosed, of which the old course was one. A particular instance involved the jockey J Fagan, on Pampas Grass. A collie ran between the horse's legs. Both horse and rider were thrown and injured, and the dog was instantly killed. Things eventually got that bad that an order was issued, that any dogs found on the course would be destroyed. A bigger menace however was caused by cabs which were allowed to cross the course to the grandstand, until one day J Grimshaw and his mount were involved in a collision, both being severely injured.

Come the late 1880's, the tack was in such a bad state of repair, plus the quality of racing so poor compared to Derby and Leicester, that the Corporation decided it could no longer support the course. The final nail in the coffin came about when an application for a drinks licence was opposed. The decision to close the course was taken at a Council Meeting in May 1890 and as you can see, it shows all the wheeling and dealing that can take place.

From copy Minutes of the a quarter Meeting of The Council held on Monday the 5th day of May 1890:

Nottingham Races.
Moved by Mr Councillor W Lee, and seconded by Mr Councillor Brownsword,

That all future Race Meetings held under the management of the Race Committee of this Corporation, there shall be no place set apart as a betting ring or enclosure, and no charge made for admission to any part of the ground under the control of the Race Committee, and that the most rigorous measures shall be adopted for the suppression of betting upon the course.

Moved by Mr Alderman Barber, by way of amendment , seconded by Alderman Sir J Turney, Kt.,

By permission of the council, Mr Councillor Lee and Mr Councillor Brownsword withdrew the motion proposed and seconded by them respectively, in favour of the amendment moved by Mr Alderman Barber.

It was then moved by Mr Councillor Bentley, and seconded by Mr Councillor Kirk,

The Last Racing Meeting September 1890

Page 53

lengths; a length and a half second and third, and a length third and fourth. 2m. 44s.

Prix de Nexon of 138l., for 2y old. 1 mi.
Hyperbole 8st 4lb ......Hartley 1
Vertu 8st 4lb ....Crickmere 2
Diligence 8st 4lb ....Cooke 8
Six ran. Even on Hyperbole, 8 to 1 agst Vertu, and 12 Diligence. Won by a length and a half ; three lengths second and third.

Prix de Cheffreville of 206l. 1 mi. 4 fur.
410 Chalet 8y 8st 11lb..Bartholomew 1
544*Wandora 3y 8st 8lb........Cooke 2
626 Yellow 8y 8st 11lb ......Hartley 8
Ihos 8y 8st 11lb ....Brigden -
6 to 1 on Wandora, 4 to 1 agst Yellow, 6½ Chalet, and 8 Ihos. Won by half a length; a length and a half second and third.

Prix de Meautry of 216l. 1 mi. 8 fur.
414 Tantale 4y 9st 4lb ......Hartley 1
412*Cameleon 4y 9st 4lb ......Lane 2
Frejeville 4y 9st 4lb ......Madge 8
Five ran. 3 to 1 agst Tantale, 2½ Cameleon, and 3 Frejeville. Won by half a length ; three lengths second and third.

NOTTINGHAM.

MONDAY, Sept. 29.—*Juvenile Plate* of 100l., for 2y old. Ab. 5 fur.
Prismoid 8st 9lb ....S. Loates 1
South Coast 8st 9lb ....Rickaby 2
583 F. by Coruleus—Restorative
8st 9lb ....A. Field 8
475 Foundling 8st 12lb ....J. Rogers -
5 to 4 on Restorative filly, 8 to 1 agst Prismoid, 4 South Coast, and 10 Foundling. Won by a length; half a length second and third.

Maiden Plate of 142l. Ab. 1 mi.
685 Aurora 2y 7st 11lb ....G. Barrett 1
544 Odd Mixture 3y 10st ....Calder 2
Elissa 8y 9st 11lb ......S. Loates 8
687 Nerissa 2y 7st 11lb...J. Woodburn -
6 to 4 each agst Aurora and Odd Mixture, 6 to 1 Elissa, and 7 Nerissa. Won by three lengths; bad third.

Bestwood Nursery Plate (H'cap) of 187l., 2y old. Ab. 5 fur.
638 Noverre 8st ....J. Watts 1
566 Crowflower 6st 13lb...R.Chaloner 2
583 Glenpairn II.6-12..Widdowfield 8
576 Rooster 6st 7lb ....C Gray -
491 Promotion 6st ....Bradford -
553*Meadow Sweet 6st 6lb..F. Peake -
Whitewood 7st 7lb.........Wall -
Even on Noverre, 100 to 30 agst Crowflower, and 100 to 8 others. Won

easily by a length and a half; four lengths second and third : Rooster fourth, Promotion fifth.

Nottinghamshire Handicap of 465l. Ab. 1 mi.
610 Glory Smitten 4y 7st 7lb T.Loates 1
632*Tommy Tittlemouse aged
8st 10lb.................Weldon 2
623 Yarm 5y 7st .. ..Mullen 8
506 Lifeguard 3y 7st 4lb Bradbury 4
600 Present Alms 4y 6-9 R. Chaloner -
495 Bonaventur- 3y 6st 8lb....Blake -
623 Oriel 4y 7st 2lb .... Allsopp -
2 to 1 agst Yarm, 8 Glory Smitten, 6 Bonaventure, 6½ Lifeguard, and 10 each Oriel,Tommy Tittlemouse, and Present Alms Won by a length ; four lengths second and third; Lifeguard fourth.

Lenton Firs Selling Plate of 100l. Ab. 5 fur.
615 Laceman aged 10st 1lb S. Loates 1
Early Dawn 3y 9st 1lb....Calder 2
608 Harpagon 5y 10st 4lb....Rickaby 8
585 Rookdale 4y 10st 4lb ...J. Watts -
584 Cylindrical 2y 8st 4lb..G.Barrett -
Even on Harpagon, 4 to 1 agst Laceman, 5 Early Dawn, and 6½ Cylindrical. Won by a neck; a length second and third; Rookdale fourth. Winner bought in for 55gs.

Elvaston Castle Stakes (H'cap) of 190l. Ab. 5 fur.
607 Grecian Bend 6y 7st 2lb Allsopp 1
606 Jack o' Lantern 6y 8-2 T. Loates 2
638 Countess Therry 5y 6st 12lb Blake 8
508 Master Charlie 4y 7-5 . Bradbury 4
931 Dame Margaret 3y 8-6..S.Loates -
633 Eider 3y 8st ....R Chaloner -
Amazon 3y 7st 4lb..Widdowfield -
579*Miss Sykes 4y 7st 1lb ...Mullen -
622*Frapotel 6y 8st 13lb ....Weldon -
623 Barberry 3y 8st..........Calder -
470 Enamel 3y 7st 1lb....J. Woodburn -
455*Pinon Altos 3y 7st ....Wall -
633 Red Cherry 3y 6st 8lb ....J Watts -
5 to 1 agst Dame Margaret, 6 each Grecian Bend and Jack o' Lantern, 8 each Eider and Master Charlie, 10 Countess Therry, 11 each Barberry, Enamel, and Miss Sykes, and 12½ Frapotel. Won by a neck; three-parts of a length second and third ; Master Charlie, close up, fourth.

Bleasby Gorse Plate (Hunters' Flat) of 72l. Ab. 1 mi.
854 Sir Hamilton 5y 12st Mr Brown 1
79 Stellaland a. 12st 1lb Mr Peacock 2
118 Telegraph 4y 11st ....Mr Sharpe 8
Melrose aged 11st 7lb Mr Bentley -
11 to 8 on Stellaland, 3 to 1 agst Sir

Hamilton, 8 Telegraph, and 10 Melrose. Won by a neck : bad third.

TUESDAY.—*Hunters' Selling Flat Race Plate* of 45l. 2 mi.
583*Martel aged 11st 7lb .. Mr Pease 1
630 Teddy aged 11st 7lb ..Mr Brown 2
630 Colchester a. 12-3 Mr Merryfield 8
11 to 10 on Martel, and 5 to 4 agst Teddy Won easily by four lengths; bad third. Winner sold to Sir W. Eden for 120gs.

Mile Nursery Plate (Handicap) of 185l., for 2y old. 1 mi.
553 Capucin 7st 7lb........S. Loates 1
624 Elsa 7st 10lb..........T Loates 2
576 Lamb's Wool 7st 4lb G.Chaloner 8
593 Purser 6st 9lb ....Blake 4
638 St. Luke 7st 2lb ....Allsopp -
644 Nerissa 6st 9lb........ Peake -
9 to 4 agst Capucin, 2½ to 1 Elsa, 8 St. Luke, 7 each Purser and Lamb's Wool, and 8 Nerissa Won by a short head; five lengths second and third; Purser fourth.

Little John Selling Plate of 100l., for old. 5 fur.
644 Rooster 8st 10lb ......T. Loates 1
623 Sunny Side 8st 10lb ....T. Loates 2
623 Early Flower 8st 10lb .. Weldon 8
9 to 4 on Rooster, 3 to 1 agst Early Flower, and 8 Sunny Side. Won easily by three-quarters of a length; three lengths second and third. Winner sold to Mr A. Day for 110gs.

Robin Hood Stakes (Handicap) of 202l. 1 mi. 4 fur.
569 Good Lad 3y 7st 13lb ....Calder 1
585 Dornoch 3y 7st 11lb..M. Cannon 2
511*Maley 3y 8st 2lb ....T. Loates 8
645 Tommy Tittlemouse aged
10st 1lb ....T. Weldon -
11 to 8 agst Maley, 100 to 30 each Good Lad and Tommy Tittlemouse, and 9 to 2 Dornoch Won by three lengths; two lengths second and third, and same third and fourth.

Welbeck Abbey Stakes (H'cap) of 190l. 6 fur.
645*Grecian Bend 6y 10lb Allsopp 1
577 Spearmint 9y 9st 1lb......Calder 2
645 Countess Therry 5y 7st 10lb
G. Barrett 8
615 Lifeguard 3y 8st 5lb...M. Cannon -
645 Martley 4y 7st ....Rickaby -
583 Althea 3y 7st 1lb ....Wall -
15 to 8 agst Martley, 8 to 1 Countess Therry, 5 each Spearmint and Grecian Bend, 7 Lifeguard, and 20 Althea. Won by a length; half a length second and third; Lifeguard fourth.

Friar Tuck Stakes of 100l., for 3y old. 1 mi.
512 Danvita 8st 7lb ....S. Loates w.o.

Sherwood H'cap Hurdle of 87l. 2 mi.
584 Purple Emperor 6y 11st 8lb
Mr Craddock 1
628*Gladstone a 10-12 A.Nightingall 2
11 to 10 on Purple Emperor. Won easily by a length.

Colgrave Gorse Plate (Hurdle) of 72l. 2 mi.
645*Sir Hamilton 5y 12st 8lb
A. Nightingall 1
889 Squire 6y 12st 4lb..Mr W. Brown 2
Ordeal 3y 10st 2lb ......Sensier 8
629 First Flight 3y 10st 2lb ..Watson -
645 Telegraph 4y 11st 2lb..Mr Sharp -
8t. Silvester 3y 10st 2lb Mr Wood -
11 to 8 agst Sir Hamilton, 13 to 8 Ordeal, and 9 to 2 Squire. Won by a head ; four lengths second and third; First Flight fourth.

The Old Grandstand On The Forest Course Shortly Before Its
Demolition In 1912

Arthur Nightingall Who Won The Last Ever Race At The Forest Track. He Won Three Grand Nationals.

"That the debate be adjourned to the next meeting of the Council." And such motion being put to the vote was defeated.

The amendment moved by Mr Alderman Barber was then put to the vote as a substantive motion, and was carried.

And the Council resolved and ordered accordingly.

On demand the votes were recorded.

The 35 members voted for the motion.

13 members voted against the motion:

Ordered on the motion of Mr Councillor Sutton, seconded by Mr Alderman J P Ford.

That the Common Seal of the Corporation be affixed by the Mayor or Deputy Mayor to the deeds and other documents set forth in the Seal Order Book, signed by the Mayor, as Chairman of this meeting.

The Meeting then dissolved.

Minutes of the Council 1889-90

The gates closed for the last time on September 30th, 1890. The last race was the Sovereign Cotgrave Gorse Plate for Hunters, which was won by Mr T Tyler's Sir Hamilton, with A Nightingale up.

Borough of Nottingham Reports Presented To The Council 1890-91

Report of The Race Committee (Appointed in November 1889)

As To The Disposal of the Funds in the Hands of That Committee

At a meeting of the Council, held on the 2nd day of February, it was in effect decided that the Races be discontinued on the present Race Course.

Without attempting in any way to reopen the question of racing on the Forest, the Committee beg to Report that some years ago, through various causes, they found themselves in difficulties, and with a considerable deficit at their Bankers. That instead of coming to the Council and asking for assistance, a few members of the

Committee agreed to accept the whole of the liabilities, and became surety for the same at the bank.

That after several years of careful management such deficit, amounting to about £1,300 was cleared off, and the profits that have since been made from time to time have been disposed of for the benefit of the inhabitants of the Borough, as for instance the lowering, levelling, and forming at great cost the Western end of the Forest, making it suitable for recreation purposes as well as for a drill ground for our volunteers, which was much needed.

That other large sums were given by the Committee in the Jubilee year to the funds of the Sunday School Union, as well as to the various Hospitals and Charities of the Town, and since then several hundreds of pounds have been handed over to the Castle Museum Committee to assist in defraying the cost of recent additions to the Castle.

That on winding up their affairs, and discharging all their liabilities, the Committee are pleased to state they have a considerable balance in their favour at the bank.

They propose disposing of the same as in former years by gifts to the Institutions, Hospitals and various Charities of the Town, in the undermentioned manner, and for which the Committee ask the Council to approve by their unanimous vote, namely:

To	the	New Technical Schools	100	0	0
To	the	Castle Museum	100	0	0
To	the	School of Art	50	0	0
To	the	General Hospital	100	0	0

To	the	General Dispensary	100 0 0
To	the	Children's Hospital	75 0 0
To	the	Women's Hospital	75 0 0
To	the	Samaritan Hospital	75 0 0
To	the	Blind Insitution	50 0 0
To	the	Eye Infirmary	50 0 0
To	the	Throat and Ear Hospital	50 0 0
To	the	Town Mission	25 0 0
To	the	Lenton Orphanage	25 0 0
To	Miss	Bailey's Orphanage	25 0 0
To	Nazareth	House	25 0 0
To	the Mayor's	Fund for Soup Kitchens	25 0 0

Dated this 23rd day of February 1891
ROBERT DENNETT CHAIRMAN

During my research I happened to come across a mention of a pantomime song of the 1890's called "Who killed Nottingham Races?". Which was sung to the tune of "Who Killed Cock Robin". The chorus went like this. "All the bookies and the backers, their hearts stopped beating, when they heard of the death of the Nottingham Meeting".

So after over 200 years, racing on The Forest came to an end. It would be nearly another two years before horse racing returned to Nottingham and like the old course there would be a fair mixture of ups and downs.

Chapter Four
The Birth of a Racecourse

The Forest After The Closure Of The Racecourse

On the 26th September 1891 there appeared in the advertising columns of the Nottingham Evening Post, an announcement that invited applications for shares in a newly floated company. The company in question was the Nottingham and Colwick (pronounced colic) Park Racecourse and Sports Company, Limited. The intention was to gain a 30 year lease from the Nottingham Contract Corporation (Limited) of the 292 Acre Colwick Park Estate for the purposes as, indicated by the title of the company. The site was inspected by Mr George Hunt who was the position of consulting surveyor to the Royal Agriculture Society of England, on whose decision to go any further was made.

NOTTINGHAM.

FRIDAY, August 19.—*Bestwood Stakes* (*H'cap*) of 255*l*. 1 mi. 3 fur.
548 Delaval 5y 8-9 ......Rickaby 1
522 Halsbury 3y 8-8 ..M.Cannon 2
558 Barmecide 6y 10-2 ..J.Watts 3
179 Red Eagle 5y 10-2..Holbeach –
523 Madame Neruda II. 4y 9-1
        C. Loates –
496 Overcast 3y 8-9 ......Weldon –
215 Sobriety 5y 8-9 ..G.Chaloner –
  11 to 4 agst Halsbury, 7 to 2 Madame Neruda II., 4 Delaval, 6 Barmecide, 10 Overcast. 16 Red Eagle. Won a length; bad third; Madame Neruda II. 4th. Overcast fell.

Friar Tuck Selling Plate of 100*l*. 1 mi.
527 Killossery 3y 8-6 G.Chaloner 1
492 Grasp 3y 8-7 ......Holbeach 2
560*Luttrellstown 3y 8-10
        M. Cannon 3
534 Drury Lane 3y 8-7 ..Rickaby –
567 Elopement II. 3y 8-7 Mullen –
  Even on Killossery, 3 to 1 agst Lut

The Results Of The First Race Meeting Of Colwick Park, August 1892. The First Race Was Won By Delaval, Ridden By Fred Rickaby (Grandfather Of Lester Piggott). Note the Long Defunct Postsmouth Park Had A Meeting On The Same Day.

trellstown, 10 Elopement II., 12½ each Drury Lane, Grasp. Won a length; half a length, Winner sold to Mr E. Weever for 380gs.

Rufford Abbey Plate of 137*l*. 6 fur.
538*Wrinkles 5y 10-0......Mullen 1
397 Hamptonian 4y 9-0
        J.Woodburn 2
466 Beecham 2y 6-11 ..G.Manser 3
  9 to 4 on Wrinkles, 11 to 4 agst Beecham, 12½ Hamptonian. Won a canter two lengths; five lengths.

Welbeck Abbey Plate (*H'cap*) of 465*l*. 5 fur.
526 Whisper 3y 7-12 G.Chaloner 1
498 Simon Renard 3y 6-7 Bradford 2
423 Day Dawn 5y 7-11 J.Woodburn 3
526 Anna 3y 6-8 ....Widdowfield 4
521 Lady Lena 3y 8-13..C. Loates –
521 Hildebert 4y 8-7......Weldon –
441 Middleham 3y 7-12 ..Allsopp –
521 Jessamy 4y 7-11 ......Finlay –
526 Scotch Earl 5y 7-6 ......Ibbett –
505 Bouthillier 3y 7-5..O.Madden –
555 Cambushinnie 3y 6-12 ..Pratt –
522 Cœlus 3y 6-10....P. Chaloner –
548 Bruree 3y 6-9 ......F. Mason –
  4 to 1 agst Simon Renard, 7 Day Dawn, 10 each Hildebert, Scotch Earl, Jessamy, Bruree, 100 to 8 each Middleham, Whisperer, 14 each Lady Lena, Bouthillier. Won three parts of a length; a head; Anna, close up, 4th, Cœlus 4th.

Oxton Selling Plate of 190*l*. 5 fur.
558 Reine des Pres 2y 8-1
        G. Chaloner 1
548 Sly Shot aged 10-4 M. Cannon 2
  Fancy 3y 9-10 ....Mullen 3
511 Juicy 2y 8-1........Bradford –
379 Juicy 2y 8-1 ....Colling –
565*Zebra 2y 8-7 ....Rickaby –
554 Torquatus 3y 9-13 ......Pratt –
552*Catch-me-Not 2y 8-4
        J.Woodburn –
  Lalage 2y 8-1 ....Finlay –
  9 to 4 agst Catch-me-Not, 4 Reine des Pres, 4½ Sly Shot, 8 Fancy. Won half a length; three-parts of a length; Gerda 4th. Winner sold to Mr H. Hyams 100gs.

Little John Plate of 177*l*., for 2y old.
  5 fur.
372 Macrame 8-2 ....S. Chandley 1
528 Simena 8-2 ....Allsopp 2
504 Melbourne 8-5....M. Cannon 3
517*Vis-a-Vis 8-9........C.Loates 4
495 Crooked Pin 8-5......Colling –

Bird's-Eye Blue 8-2 ..Mullen –
497 Scottish Maiden 8-2
        J.Woodburn –
  Gabrielle 8-2..........Finlay –
  6 to 4 agst Simena, 9 to 4 Macrame, 6 Melbourne, 8 Scottish Maiden, 10 Vis-a-Vis. Won a canter four lengths; a length; Vis-a-Vis 4th.

SATURDAY.—*Robin Hood Plate* of 137*l*., for 2y old. 5 fur.
576 Scottish Maiden 8-9
        J.Woodburn 0
  Halma 8-9...........G.Chaloner 0
478 Saints' Day 8-9 ......Colling 3
575 Melbourne 8-12....M.Cannon –
473 Gill Beck 8-9 ....Weldon –
  F. by Charibert—Miss Mabel
  8-9..................Allsopp –
  Cachuca 8-9 ....Finlay –
  5 to 2 agst Melbourne, 3 Halma, 4 Scottish Maiden, 7 Naughty Lass, 8 Gill Beck. Dead heat; third three lengths off; Gill Beck 4th. Stakes divided.

Lenton Firs Handicap of 100*l*. 5 fur.
288 Gloss 3y 8-9....... M.Cannon 1
543 Carlina 3y 8-2 ....Bradford 2
467 Ruwenzori 3y 8-18 G.Chaloner 3
568*Towton 3y 9-9 ....Finlay –
515 Ordinance 4y 8-13......J.Watts –
496 Trojan 3y 8-13 .. J.Woodburn –
  9 to 4 agst Ruwenzori, 8 each Towton and Gloss, 8 Trojan, 10 Carlina, 12½ Ordinance. Won a length and a half; three-parts of a length; Ordinance 4th.

Sherwood Selling Plate of 100*l*. 6 fur.
501*C. by Highborn—Jew's Harp
  2y 8-0...........S. Chandley 1
575 Juicy 2y 7-8 ....J.Woodburn 2
575 Torquatus 3y 9-8 ..M.Cannon 3
546 Ochone 2y 7-7 ....Bradford –
  2 to 1 agst Jew's Harp colt, 2½ each Torquatus and Juicy, 5 Ochone. Won two lengths; same. Winner bought in 170gs.

Nottinghamshire H'cap of 925*l*. 1 mi.
516*Golden Garter 4y 8-13
        J.Woodburn 1
539 Glory Smitten 6y 8-10 M.Cannon 2
438 Breach 4y 9-0 ....Finlay 3
521 Kentigern 4y 7-8 S.Chandley 4
470 Patrick Blue 4y 8-13 J.Watts –
526 Haymaker 3y 8-4 ..Bradford –
179 Dorice 4y 9-0 ....Colling –
462 Mr McGregor 5y 7-10 Mullen –
541 Knockany 3y 7-11 G.Chaloner –
496 Vampire 3y 7-8....O.Madden –

472 Fandango 3y 7-5 ....Allsopp –
  9 to 2 agst Breach, 5 Golden Garter, 6 each Patrick Blue, Knockany, 8 Mr M'Gregor, 9 Kentigern, 12½ Vampire, 14 Glory Smitten, 20 each Haymaker, Dorice, Fandango. Won two lengths; same; Dorice 5th. Knockany 6th.

Portland Plate (*Handicap*) of 187*l*.
  1 mi.
512 Ravenspur 3y 10-2 M.Cannon 1
160 Royal Princess 3y 9-9 Weldon 2
  2 to 1 on Ravenspur. Won easily three lengths.

Colwick Park Selling Plate of 141*l*., for 2y old. 5 fur.
555 Lomond 8-10 ....Colling 1
5:5 Naughty Girl 8-7 G.Chaloner 2
575*Reine des Pres 8-11M.Cannon 3
575 Zebra 9-0...........Rickaby –
575 Gerda 8-7 ....J.Woodburn –
575 Catch-me-Not 8-11
        J. Woodburn –
  5 to 4 on Naughty Girl, 9 to 4 agst Reine des Pres, 8 Catch-me-Not, 10 Lomond. Won a head; length and a half; Catch-me-Not 4th. Winner sold to Major Wickham 180gs.

Elvaston Castle Plate of 197*l*. 1 mi.
576 Kentigern 4y 9-3 S Chandley w.o.

PORTSMOUTH PARK.
[Course on the soft side.]

FRIDAY, August 19.—*Maiden Plate* of 100*l*., for 2y old. 5 fur.
  C. by Lammermoor—
  Carrara 9-0.....J.Liddiard 1
  Philadelphus 9-0 ..G.Barrett 2
  Sparkenhoe 9-0 ..Tomlisson 3
  Mary Langden 8-11 Griffiths –
  F. by Westburton—
  Ladybird 8-11........Peake –
  Preston 9-0 ....Wall –
  Silver Cord 8-11...A.Watts –
353 Lady Toto 8-11 ......A.Watts –
  Lord Montague 9-0 .. Martin –
412 C. by Frontier, dam by
  Plebeian 9-0 ..Mr Thirlwell –
551 Careysville 9-0 ..Edmondson –
  3 to 1 agst Carrara colt, 4 Sparkenhoe, 4½ Philadelphus, 6 Careysville. Won a canter a length and half; four length; Careysville 4th.

Fratton Handicap of 100*l*. 5 fur.
531 Admiral Benbow aged 7-11
        G. Barrett 1
481*Stop 4y 7-8 ....Harper 2
551 Florence 3y 7-9......Griffiths 3
498*Gold Reef 4y 9-2 ....Anthony –

The share capital was £35,000, divided into shares of £1 each paid in the following proportions 5 shillings to be paid upon application, 5 shillings upon allotment of the shares, and the remaining 10 shillings before the 1st March 1892. The Earl of Harrington of Elvaston Castle, who was also Master of the South Notts. Hunt, headed the list of directors. Which also included Major Egerton, Mr G.E.Jarvis, Alderman William Lambert J.P, and Alderman R.Denett. The long connection with the Ford family was continued as Mr W. Ford was company Secretary, while his father Mr W.J.Ford was Clerk of the Course and stakeholder. The starter was Mr Aubrey Coventry. The list for anyone wishing to subscribe opened on Monday 5th October 1891 and closed the following Saturday on the 10th October. The directors had not left things to chance, as they had already been granted a licence by the Jockey Club to hold six days of flat racing. While there was significant hope to hold racing under National Hunt Rules.

Colwick Park is about 1½ miles east of the city centre. Over ninety years after the grand opening, Aylwin Sampson aptly describes the setting of the track in his book Courses of Action published by Hale in 1984. *'It is Colwick Hill that acts as the backcloth to the scene, any encroachment by building must be resisted for there are not many racecourses with so fine a feature a mile or so from the city centre.'*

Due to the close proximity of Colwick Park to the centre of Nottingham, the racecourse was well served by many modes of transport as in an article from the Nottingham Evening Post dated 11th August 1892: *'The course is approached by a wide sweeping road, which extends from the old lane past the entrance for the main body of the public, down to the inlets for the club and Tattersall's members, and which has been specially constructed by the Racecourse Company. It is just at the commencement of this road that the Great Northern Railway Company will discharge passengers, who will be able to leave the station and at once enter at the turnstiles, six of which have been provided'.*

At the six furlong marker there was a special siding yet again built by the Great Northern Railway for the unloading of the horses, where it was but a 100 yard walk across the course to their stables behind the magnificent Colwick Hall (now a hotel and a shadow of it's former glory). The arrangement as regards the transportation of the horses, which was a vast improvement on the order of things, when there was racing on The Forest. Because the nearest train station was Victoria (now the site of the Victoria Centre) and many a time there was lines of horses being led up Mansfield Road through the heavy traffic.

Although the train line was provided by Great Northern, further services was provided by Midland, London, North Western, as well as the Nottingham and District Suburban Railway Companies. The transport was aided by a steamboat service on the River Trent, return fare was 3d. Three steamers were used, Sunbeam, Queen and Empress. The Sunbeam was sold to Leicester Fire Brigade in 1941, for a fire float. While the Empress was built in 1879 and ended her days at Dunkirk in 1940.

As already mentioned the stables were situated behind Colwick Hall. There being 42 boxes in all. Each had all the latest mod cons of the time.

The first time the majority of the general public, get to see the horses is around the paddock, which is ably described by the Nottingham Evening Post of 11th August 1892.

'On the right of the large stand, beneath which have been built all the offices entrances for members will be found the paddock, which is not only large but well sheltered by trees, which in hot weather will keep out the sun, and in wet the rain. Upon the sloping bank at the Nottinghamside seats will be placed, so that ladies will find this a very pleasant ground for a rest from the bustle and heat of racing. The horses too will be able to walk round without danger to spectators, as is the case where one enclosure has to serve for both ring, paddock, and sales.'

The Evening Post goes onto comment about the Weighing room and press building, which at the time were considered on a par with any course in the country.

'At the connecting gate between the paddock and the base of the course, the weighing room has been built, a commodious one-storey building, with a flat roof upon which will be found accommodation for members of the press and trainers. From here a magnificent view can be obtained of the whole of the course straight and round, and as admirable rooms have been constructed below for press, clerk of the scales, stewards, jockeys, gentlemen riders, there ought to be no overcrowding or inconvenience. The Club and Tattersalls enclosures were one and separate. In that although they

were separate entities, there was their own different parts of the main stand. Being 56 yards long, it was divided equally between the two enclosures. It provided excellent viewing from no matter which part you happened to be in. However in front of the Club, there was a railed off square, solely for the steward's use.

The Silver Ring stand, as expected less cellubious than the main stand, it was still an imposing structure in it's own right. Forty yards long it consisted of 15 tiers of seats. Making it that the rings were capable of holding in excess of 4,000 people.

Underneath each stand, there was bars provided for the patrons. While the Club and Tattersalls had separate restaurants, as well as private rooms set aside for luncheons and parties.

At the Silver Ring end of Tattersalls, there was a telegraph office, with the provision of four quadruplex instruments. For use by either patrons of the Silver Ring Tattersalls or Members while the most popular users must have been the press'

The layout of the track is fairly simple, no different to any other course. The flat course is 1½ miles in circumference. It is frequently used by Newmarket trainers an introductory run for their promising two-year-olds.

Up until 1965 mile races were run on the straight course, which was generally considered one of the fairest tests of a Thoroughbred. However not everyone was in total agreement F.H.Bayles in his excellent The Race Courses of Great Britain and Ireland, does not mince his words about a slight rise in the ground at the four furlong marker.

F. RICKABY

Fred Rickaby: Rode Delaval The First Ever Winner
At Colwick Park.

'The mile seven, six and five furlongs are perfectly straight, and may be considered as absolutely identical with the straight course at Lingfield in every particular. There is a swell in the ground, as if a watercourse ran under it, about halfway to the winning post, calculated to put horses out of their stride.

I suggest that no bulge should be allowed to exist on any race-course, because, though it may not be everyone's opinion, *nothing is more calculated to make a horse change it's legs or lose it's natural stride.'*

As well as the infamous bulge, horses also had to negotiate two roads for use by carts, on the straight mile, however before the days racing they were covered by ashes. If that was not enough 130 yards from the winning post, there was a five foot wide footpath, for the use by spectators who wished to gain access to the centre of the course.

Bayles went onto describe the chase course as thus; 'The *Steeple Course is partly inside , and finishes on the flat course. The brush fences are of birch, small, and very upright and easy. The guard rail to the deep ditch is unbanked. The brook is facing the stand. The going is very good in fair, but deep and holding in bad weather.*

A very awkward angle occurs in the course, jockeys should avoid the rails by keeping as near as possible to the centre of he course, which will bring them in nearly a direct line with the winning -post, otherwise they lose ground after taking the last fence, and are liable to be shut in at the very curious bend, which occurs on the final run-in, about 150 yards from home.'

The curious bend referred to on the run-in, was the water jump which used to be in front of the stands, till it was moved to the far side of the course in about 1948.

The run-in to the inaugural meeting of August 19th and 20th 1892, raised the hopes and expectations of the racecourse executive; no doubt due to the large number of entries received for the two feature races which were the Nottingham and Welbeck handicaps.

Chapter Five
Up and Running

Colwick Park racecourse opened it's gates to the public on 19th August 1892. While there happened to be a general election at the time, they still managed to attract a fair sized crowd in terms of both quantity and quality. The quality was exemplified by Lord's Rosslyn and Newark, Major and Lady Eleanor Wickham. Major Egerton, General Duncombe and the aforementioned Sir George Chetwynd. While also in attendance was the Lord Mayor of Nottingham Mr.R.Fitzhugh.

Owners with runners included the likes of the Duke of Portland, Lord's Randolph Churchill (father of Sir Winston Churchill), Hastings and Zetland.

The day started with the Bestwood Stakes worth 250 sovereigns for three-year-olds and upwards over 1 mile, 3 furlongs and resulted in a one-two for Lester Piggott's ancestors. In that Fred Rickaby on Mr Sibary's Delaval beat Mr Abingdon's Halsbury with Mornington Cannon up. Fred Rickaby was Lester's grandfather.

The main race the Welbeck Abbey Plate fell to the complete outsider in Mr H.McCalmont's Whisperer ridden by G.Chaliner, who had the honour of riding Colwick Park's first treble. The treble was initiated in the Friar Tuck Selling Plate by Captain Machell's Killossery trained by James Jewitt, two forthright and brilliant men who clashed more than once, usually over the running of Triple Crown hero Isinglass. The treble was completed when he rode his fathers Reine Des Pres to victory in the Oxton Selling Plate. Just three runners turned out for the Rufford Abbey Plate in which the 9-4 on favourite Wrinkles a five year old owned by Mr Brechin and ridden by Millen won from the four year old Hamponian owned by Tom Jenning's Jnr, whose father trained the 1865 Triple Crown and Grand Prix de Paris winner Gladiateur "The Avenger" of Waterloo. Who the following year won the Ascot Gold Cup by 20 lengths. (A descendant of the famed Jenning's is the former I.T.V. racing presenter John Rickman). The day ended with the Little John Plate over five furlongs for two-year-olds, in which Mr J. Hutchinson's Macrame ridden by S. Chandley, made all the running to win by four lengths from Simene with Melbourne a length away in third.

If the Friday was success it still paled in comparison to the Saturday. Although a bumper crowd was anticipated, it still exceeded the executive expectations; as the attendance was estimated somewhere in the region of 30,000. Much of it due to the weather which was the same as the day before, brilliant sunshine. The racecourse station was best described by the Nottingham Daily Guardian of Monday August 22nd 1892:-
"Numerous special trains were run by the Great Northern and London and North-Western Railway Companies to the racecourse station, where between 70 and 80 trains stopped during the day, and the quick service of local trains from the Great Northern Station to the racecourse was very convenient, though the carriages were crowded. The Midland Railway Company also gave special facilities for passengers attending the meeting and in this connection it may

be remarked that the railway officials have exerted themselves admirably to secure the success of the gathering".

The opening race was the five furlong Robin Hood Plate for two-year-olds, which witnessed a dead-heat between Mr.R.Batterill's Scottish Maiden and Captain Machell's Halma (formerly known as Prince Bismark) ridden by G.Chaliner, so making it his fourth winner of the meeting. After a hastily arranged meeting between the winning connections it was decided to split the stakes, in so doing there became no need for a run off.

The following race was the Lenton Firs Plate yet again over five furlongs, but this time for three-year-olds and upwards. To say the least though it was an uneventful race, with the exception of the first ever Colwick Park winner for that great jockey and horseman Mornington Cannon. This he acheived on Sir.C.Hartog's Gloss. He was then reigning champion jockey and got his unusual name when his father Tom won at Bath on the day of his son's birth 21st May 1873, the horse was of course called Mornington.

Just four horses turned out for the Sherwood Selling Plate, which saw S.Chandly ride Captain Percy Bewicke's Jew's Harp to victory. Captain Bewicke was a rider of some distinction under National Hunt rules, in which he was leading amateur of 1891 and 92. He later went onto train with varying success, but when he retitred in 1927 he said "I shall not mind if I see a racecourse again".

The day's big race, the Nottinghamshire Handicap worth 1000 sovereigns, over the straight mile, saw the recently knighted Sir Blundell Maple's, Golden Garter win. In so doing completed a double for jockey J.Woodburn. He was a popular winner with the punters as he started 5-1 2nd favourite. Two lengths back in second was Glory Smitten owned and trained by Joe Cannon, while ridden by his more illustrious brother Mornington, Joe Cannon's main owner was George Baird, the leading amateur rider of the 1880's, who raced under the name of Mr Abingdon, but was known universally as The Squire. While he owned Merry Hampton who won the 1887 Derby on his debut, it gave him little if any pleasure, so much so he refused to lead in the horse after he won. Where he did gain his racing kicks from was riding a winner. even to the extent of paying the owner-trainer and jockey for the ride, something that helped him ride a still seasonal record for an amateur of 61 winners, which he gained in 1887. Apart from that his other main claim to fame was the lover of the renowned victorian "Lady" Lillie Langtry. However it was not just his affections that he lavished on her. After one particular bruising encounter in Paris he gave her £50,000 and a yacht called Whyte Lady, but everyone called Black Eye.

After the eleven runner Nottinghamshire Handicap there was just the two for the Portland Plate, From an original entry of fourteen, things have still not changed. The race went to the 2-1 on favourite Ravenspur so completing a double for Mornington Cannon.

The Colwick Park Selling Plate for two-year-olds over five furlongs saw Mr W.Taylor's Sharpe's, Lomond in the hands of

R. W. Colling make all the running to win by a head: The meeting ended on a downward note when just one turned-out for the Elvaston Castle Plate, which went to Colonel Heywood's Kentigern who ran earlier in the day, in the main event.

For some reason best known at the time, the new Nottingham course was generally called "The Kempton Of The Midlands". After the roaring success of the innaugural meeting, particularly the Saturday, things looked well for the future. Two more days flat racing of comparitively modest fare were held in October. Because of overcrowding especially in the Silver Ring, the directors took the decision to relplace the existing stand, which was all of one year old. The new one was able to hold 6,000 people, and stood until April 1984.

The Jockey Club took the decision to grant them a further two days racing, for their second year making a total of six. This was more than doubled to fifteen for 1894. Steeplechasing first put in an appearance at Colwick in 1893.

The first race under National Hunt Rules took place there on Monday 27th and was given the title of A Selling National Hunt Flat Race, it was the third race of a mixed seven race card. Run over two miles, it was won by Mr C.J.Robinson's Silver Cloud, ridden by Mr Westerby. Four lengths back in second was Lord Shrewsbury's Ding Dong. After the race Lord Shrewsbury objected to the winner on the grounds that Mr Westaby was not qualified to ride. I imagine that this was due to some doubt which existed about his status as an amateur. An accusation that has often been levelled at Gentleman Riders down the ages. In that it is just not their attitude to race-riding which is proffessional. The objection was subsequently dropped. According to a report at the time the third horse Mr Tyler's Puergere was only allowed to run when under Rule 34, the usual fee of £5 was paid.

Forty minutes later at 3.50 followed the day's big race the Nottingham Spring Handicap of 1,000 sovereigns over the straight mile. After three false starts, Kentigern who ran with some distinction at the innaugural meeting back in August was quickly away, and soon established a lead from Opponent and Sallaputty (names still have not improved that much), Prince Hampton was in rear. But with two furlongs left to run the two pacesetters Kentigern and Dazzle faded while Juvenal held the late surge of Prince Hampton by two lengths. The winner was owned by Mr D Cooper and ridden by F.Allsopp. While the runner-up was owned by Sir John Blundell Maple and ridden by John Watts, who three years later was to gain immortallity by riding the Prince of Wales later King Edwards VII's Persimmon to victory in the Derby and St Leger. Watts (whose great grandson is Bill Watts of Teleprompter fame) was never the happiest of looking man, mainly due to his incessant wasting. Even after he won the Derby of 1896 on Persimmon he was looking that solemn, it caused Royal Trainer Richard Marsh to slap him on the thigh, and say *'cheer up you've just won the Derby for the Prince of Wales,'* only then did he raise a flicker of a smile. Incidentally according to contempory reports Juvenile set a record time of 1 minute 38 1/5 seconds for the English Mile.

The final race on the card, was the Trent Hurdle Race over 2 miles which was won by Mr W. Blake's Romeo with Arthur

Nightingall up. Apart from riding the last winner on the old Nottingham Course he will go down in racing history as the rider of three Grand National winners in Ilex (1890), Why Not (1894) and Grudon (1901). The fashion at that time was for steeplechase riders to lean right back in the saddle, especially over the drop fences at Aintree, and Nightingall happened to be the leading exponent of this particular art.

The racing at Nottingham on March 28th lacked both the quality and quantity of the previous day. To say the least the races provided nothing to write home about. However the last race, the 2 mile Oxton H'cap Hurdle had two notable exceptions. One being a visitor from across the Irish Sea in Mr Dunne's De Beers. Although he was a well backed 9'4 favourite he could only finish last of eleven runners. While at the other end of the field, it proved a triumphant return for Colwick Park's first ever winner Delaval owned by Mr Sibary. This time ridden by Arthur Nightingall, the race was a family success for that great racing family the Nighingall's as the winner was trained by Arthur's brother William. Their father John trained two Grand National winners in Shifnal (1878) and Llex (1890). While William's son Walter trained with great success for Dorothy Paget and Sir Winston Churchill..

Colwick Park's first ever all National Hunt Card, took place three days later on Easter Saturday April 1st. A day that did not pass without some topical amusements, as we shall see later. The day dawned fine and sunny although by the afternoon it was overcast and dull. The opening race was the Bestwood Hurdle Race Plate over two miles which went to Captain H.R.Purefoy's

Fair Edith ridden by D. Shanahan. The third race on the card was the first ever steeplechase run there which went under the title of the Colwick Selling Steeplechase. The winner being Mr Deepridge's Poacher with F.Lawton up, who beat Mr Thompson's High Priest ridden by his owner, a length.

It was originally intended to be a seven race card, although in the end, only six races took place. The reason for this, was that the fifth race on the card was declared void. Of the original nine entries for the appropiately named Fool Steeplechase not one bothered to turn up, as you can imagine it caused a fair amount of amusement. It should be mentioned that at this particular time there was no such thing as overnight declarations, that did not come about until the late 1950's. A trainer could leave it as short as half an hour before the time of the said race, to declare his horse. Which no doubt caused a great deal of confusion to the on-course betting market, let alone the off-course back street bookies.

Many of National Hunt's early meetings went under various titles for various reasons. Ususally because they were run by some local hunt and on similar lines to the bona-fide Hunt Meetings that came into existance in the early years of the Twentieth Century, (a cross between a point-to-point and racing under National Hunt Rules). Nottingham's second all jumps meeting was no exception to this which took place on Monday 8th May. It being the south Notts Hunt who four days earlier had had a meeting at Hazelford Ferry.The opening race at Colwick Park was the Castle Selling Steeplechase Plate and went to the 11-10 favourite Salmon Fry owned by Mr .H.Dann and ridden by

Mr Harper, who made all the running to win by fifteen lengths. At the subsequent auction, there must have been a great deal of interest from prosepective buyers, as connections had to go to 130 guineas to buy him back in. This considering that the race was only worth 40 sovereigns.

The meeting also featured two non-events. The first being the Harrington Steeplechase Plate over 3 miles. Which had a heavily backed red-hot favourite at 5-2 on in Mr Frank Godson's Arran. Who when in second place to the long time leader and eventual winner Mr Brereton Haye's Smerby with only half a mile left to run, the favourite ran out. I imagine it caused more delight to the bookmakers than the punters. However saying that it wouldn't have taken much money for Arran's S.P. to be 5-2 on at what was no more than a small country meeting. Although he could'nt have been to happy in carrying 13 stone compared to the other two runners 11st 12lbs. Eventually Arran rejoined the race to finish a distant third.

The following race on the card, the Bestwood Steeplechase Plate over two miles, was literally a non-event, in that it was declared void yet again because of the original entries none were declared to run.

At the early meetings, there were a couple of 'natural' jumps similar to those still in place at Punchestown on the steeplechase course.

In the formative years of Colwick Park Racecourse the best horse to appear there either flat or national hunt, was the dual

Grand National winner Manifesto (1897 &99). Who until the advent of Red Rum in the mid 1970's was the supreme master of Aintree. Over a ten year period Manifesto's Grand National record reads ,1895, 4th, 1896 fell, 1897 won, 1899 won under a joint record winning weight of 12st 7lb. The first year of the twentieth century saw him lump the crushing burden of 12st 13lb into 3rd place, only giving way up that long run-in. He was to finish third again in 1902 under 12st 8lb and on his seasonal debut to boot, something which now would be unthinkable. This was the first time in public he was ridden by Ernie Piggott, grandfather to Lester. He completed his hat-trick of third's in the 1903 running under 12st 3lb. His final Grand National outing was in 1904 in which he was unplaced carrying 12st 1lb as a sixteen year old.

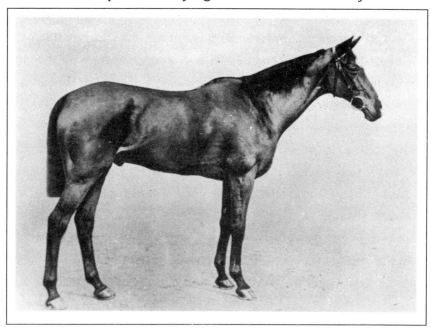

Manifesto: Grand National winner (1897 And 1899)

Going back to his Nottingham run though, and it was no more than that. It was in the 2 mile Great Midland Handicap Chase worth £405 (a prize highly valued at the time) on December 21st 1896. In what was his first outing of the season he carried 12st 7lb and was ridden for the only time in his career by W.Hoyston. However he was unquoted in the betting and uplaced in the race behind Ebor.

So you might say it was a case of schooling in public. It was to be another 34 years before a horse of comparable ability appeared at Nottingham: Golden Miller.

One final thing about Manifesto. When that great equine artist Emile Adam was asked to paint the horse's portrait, after his second National win, Adam flatly turned the offer down and he almost considered it an insult, as he did not wish to waste his talents on a mere chaser. But after a great deal of persuassion he eventually accepted the commission.On seeing Manifesto he said in amazement "why this is a racehorse!".

The Nottingham and Colwick Park Race Course and Sports Company, Limited.

FIRST ANNUAL MEETING.

Directors.

ALDERMAN W. LAMBERT, J.P., Chairman.

THE RT. HON. THE EARL OF HARRINGTON.   G. E. JARVIS, ESQ.

MAJOR EGERTON.   G. DUNCOMBE, ESQ.

R. DENNETT, ESQ.

....

The Directors have pleasure in presenting their Report and Statement of Accounts from the formation of the Company to the 30th November, 1892.

Your Directors are pleased to state that the First Race Meeting was held on the 19th and 20th August last, and proved in every way most successful. A Second Meeting was held in October, which was also very satisfactory.

The Race Course has met with the fullest approval of Owners and Trainers of Race Horses, and of Jockeys and others connected with Racing.

At the First Meeting it was found that the 2s. 6d. Ring set out for 4,000 persons was quite insufficient, so it has been enlarged to accommodate 6,000. It has also been necessary to erect additional Stabling to take in 38 more horses, making altogether Boxes for 79 horses, with Rooms for Stable Boys.

The Cycle Track has been completed, and it is hoped will next season be largely used.

A Six days' License for Colwick Hall to be used as an Hotel has been granted by the County Licensing Justices, and the Directors are now considering the best way of dealing with it.

The Great Northern Railway Company have erected a Siding and Station adjoining the Race Course, and have liberally met the views of your Directors in providing train service for those attending the Races, which will greatly add to the interests of the Shareholders of the Race Company.

The Accounts show a profit of £682 12s. 5d., which the Directors consider very encouraging, as the two meetings have both been held within the last few months, and the Expenditure covers a period of Fourteen months.

The Directors recommend that after the payment of their fees, the balance of profit be carried to next year's account.

The Auditor, Mr. H. E. Hubbart retires, and offers himself for re-election.

W. LAMBERT, *Chairman.*

R. DENNETT.

W. FORD, *Secretary.*

3rd December, 1892.

Page 80

THE NOTTINGHAM AND COLWICK PARK RACE COURSE AND SPORTS COMPANY, Limited.

BALANCE SHEET, November 30th, 1892.

Liabilities.

	£ s. d.	£ s. d.
To NOMINAL CAPITAL		35,000 0 0
,, Subscribed Capital, 34,982 Shares at £1 each...	34,982 0 0	
Less Calls unpaid...	825 0 0	
		34,157 0 0
,, The Contract Corporation, balance of purchase...		1353 3 4
,, Amounts due for extensions of works estimated at...		2070 0 0
,, Sundry Creditors		555 10 0
,, Balance of Revenue account ...		682 12 5
		£38,818 5 9

Assets.

	£ s. d.	£ s. d.
By LEASEHOLD, STANDS, BUILDINGS, &c.		28,407 12 0
,, Additions and Extras on Building contract		2070 0 0
,, Furniture, Fixtures, and Fittings ...	503 13 3	
,, Loose Plant ...	91 3 2	
,, Farm Implements ...	56 2 9	
		650 19 2
,, Preliminary Expenses	156 8 6	
Less written off	19 11 1	
		136 17 5
,, Sundry Debtors ...		574 4 1
,, Cash at Bank ...	6968 18 2	
,, Cash in hand ...	9 14 11	
		6978 13 1
		£38,818 5 9

I certify that the above Balance Sheet is correct, and in my opinion fairly states the position of the Company as at November 30th, 1892.

Dated the 3rd day of December, 1892.

H. E. HUBBART,

Chartered Accountant,

10, South Parade, Nottingham.

THE NOTTINGHAM AND COLWICK PARK RACE COURSE AND SPORTS COMPANY, Limited.

....

PROFIT AND LOSS ACCOUNT

From the formation of the Company, to November 30th, 1892.

Dr.   **Cr.**

	£	s.	d.		£	s.	d.
To Rent, Rates, Taxes and Insurance	1387	4	10	By Profits on Race Meetings, August, 1892, and October, 1892 ...	2336	12	4
,, Salaries and Wages ...	287	14	0				
,, Repairs and Maintenance ...	104	7	10	,, Rents ...	234	1	1
,, Sundry Expenses ...	181	19	11	,, Bank Interest	107	11	6
,, Advertising, Printing and Stationery	54	4	6	,, Transfer Fees and Sundry Receipts	7	11	6
,, Stamps and Telegrams ...	13	11	3	,, Club Account, £ s. d.			
,, Commission on Forfeits ...	2	10	0	Subscriptions ... 320 5 0			
,, Professional and other charges ...	187	9	10	Day Tickets ... 45 15 0			
,, Bank Commission ...	41	15	0		366	0	0
,, Interest on purchase money ...	73	5	9				
,, Bad Debts reserve on outstanding forfeits ...	15	10	0				
,, Proportion of Preliminary Expenses written off ...	19	11	1				
,, Profit on two meetings held ...	682	12	5				
	£3051	16	5		£3051	16	5

To Directors' Fees   By Balance Profit brought down   £682 12 5

W. LAMBERT, *Chairman.*
R. DENNETT.
W. FORD, *Secretary.*

THE

Nottingham and Colwick Park

Race Course & Sports Coy.,

LIMITED.

FIRST REPORT OF DIRECTORS
And BALANCE SHEET,

TO 30th NOVEMBER, 1892.

NOTICE IS HEREBY GIVEN that the ORDINARY GENERAL MEETING of THE NOTTINGHAM AND COLWICK PARK RACE COURSE AND SPORTS COMPANY, LIMITED, will be held at COLWICK HALL, Colwick, near Nottingham, on SATURDAY, the 17th day of DECEMBER, 1892, at 11 a.m., for the following purposes :—To transact the ordinary business of the Company. To receive the Directors' Report. To consider the Accounts. To fix the Directors' Remuneration. To elect an Auditor in place of the one retiring.

NOTICE IS HEREBY FURTHER GIVEN that the Transfer Books of the Company will be closed from the 9th December to the 19th December, 1892, both days inclusive.

Dated this 8th day of December, 1892.

By Order of the Board,

WILLIAM FORD,

Secretary.

Bromley Place,
Nottingham.

FORMAN AND SONS, NOTTINGHAM.

Chapter Six
The Edwardian Years

By the early Twentieth Century Nottingham had already found it's own little niche in the hierachy of racecourses. As best described by Charles Richardson in his The English Turf, A Record of Horses and Courses published by Methuen & Co in 1901:- *'Though so near the river the course is on sound, well drained old turf, and is generally very good going. The programmes are of a good second-rate sort. Not the best of class is seen here, nor yet the worst, the happy medium being well, both with regard to prizes and to the average class of runners. There are some capitol cross-country prizes during the winter, and the place, popular with owners, trainers, and the general public,is on the high road to success, both financially and from a racing point of view.'*

One of the biggest problems facing racing today is the amount of non-triers. However this is nothing compared to how it was in the sport's formative years, particularly over the sticks.

So at the turn of the century the National Hunt Commitee took the decision to crackdown on this un-wanted, practise. Many of the game's top names fell by the way-side. One such notable was Triple Grand National winning trainer Tom Couthwaite who was warned off for thirty years .

Such a fate almost befell leading jockey Percy Woodland, who rode with equal success under both codes. Winning the Grand National's of 1903 & 13 on Drumcree and Covercout, also the

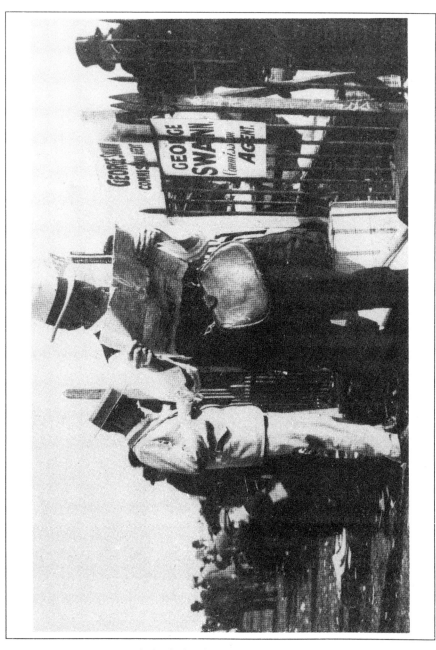

Rails Bookmakers At Colwick In 1908

French Derby with Maintenon in 1906 and Or du Rhin (1910). As well as being Champion N/H Jockey in 1903.

The two races concerned were the January H'cap Hurdle at Hurst Park on Januuary 14th 1911 in which he finished nowhere. And the Harrington H'cap Hurdle at Nottingham on January 30th 1911 which he won by five lengths starting a 7-4 favourite, the horse concerned was Wild Aster. After this race at Nottingham, he was called in by the local stewards and warned as to his future conduct. The question of non triers has been with us for a long time.

As was to be expected racing suffered under the war restrictions. Although it did manage to survive, but on a drastically reduced scale. For instance the Derby was run on Newmarket's July Course, while Gatwick played host to the Grand National, and this was after a good deal of heated argument at Westminster and in the press. As large sections of both politicians and public felt that the transport of racehorses during wartime would place an unneccessary strain on resources. To say nothing that it was also considered to be in bad taste for people to be enjoying themselves at the races, whilst our brave soldiers were putting life and limb at risk.

Balanced against this, was the boost it would give to public moral. Something to help them take their minds of the horrors of war for an hour or two. While there was also the future of the thoroughbred to consider, this obviously applies just to flat racing.A lapse in horse racing for a significant period of time, could cause a chasm in the breeding industry, as the racecourse

An Oyster Stall At Colwick Park In 1908

is the arena for future mares but especially stallions.

Like many a racecourse in the land Nottingham was requisitioned for military purposes. In Colwick Park's case it was for the South Notts Hussars, who started their training operations there in October 1914, and did not leave until the last day of February 1915.

This permitted racing to take place a month later on March 29th. The day certainly provided a wide variety of weather as apart from the much loved sun, there was also some snow.

In the Nottingham Evening Post of that day, the racing headlines read:- The Khaki Jacket, interesting incident at Colwick races, and Mapperley among the winners. So the racing was if nothing else incident packed.

The opening race was the Colwick Selling Race for 3 year olds and up over five furlongs. Just as the names for this race were going up in the numbers board, the course saw an influx of punters. Many whom were wounded soldiers out for the day. As reports suggest they were more than glad to see some racing. The race went to the joint oldest horse at nine years of age Mr W Dixon's Wamba II the 4-5 favourite.While the other nine year old in the field and second favourite at 9-4 Canonite, whipped around at the start and was left. In third place was Mr J Bennett's Money Bag, whose jockey C Foy wore a khaki jacket. The was brought in by his Winchester trainer Arnold for 80 guineas.

The second event on the card was the, Little John Plate for 2 year olds also over 5 furlongs.In which some more punters were forced to leave their money at the start. When this time, the heavily backed 2-1 favourite. Stanley Wooliton's Cannon Ball Colt. Racing was then still very much in the dark ages, in that horses were allowed to run un-named. Albeit only during their two-year-old season. The race went to Sir John Rovinson's Mapperley who provided coincedence backer's with a little windfall.As both Arnold (trainer of the first race winner) and Mapperley are adjacent areas of North Nottingham. Sir John Robinson was owner of the Worksop Manor stud, his family's fortune derived from the local brewery Home Ales.

Deformed was a popular choice with backers at 9-4, for the Trent Selling Plate. On the basis that he would be fit as a butchers dog, as he had been hurdling. He had been entered by his owner, to be sold win or lose and after finishing fifth, he was sold to a Mr T.Edge for 60 guineas. The race itself, was the most exciting of the day.For after a stirring battle Fairlight managed to overhaul Le Touquet by a short head, with 3/4 length to the third Bill Smoggens. So depriving Le Touquet's jockey Wing of a Selling race double. The winner was bought in for 190 guineas.

The day's main race was the Nottingham Spring H'cap, over 1 mile 2 furlongs, worth £437. Favourite at 2-1 was Early Hope, who the time before. had finished seventh in the Lincoln. Next best in the betting at 5-2 came Carancho, who was hoping to fulfill the promise he showed last season, when he was considered to have a fair chance in the Derby. Second he was in the betting and he occupied the same place in the race. As the winner by a neck was the Walter Griggs ridden Fruitlands, who raced the previous season as Saint Cyr.

This was one race where the tension was thoroughly maintained, as there was an objection by the rider of the second, Foy, to the winner for crossing. The objection though was overuled and the £5 deposit was lost.

The day's last two races were not particularly enthralling encounters. The Rufford Abbey H'cap and the Clifton Plate were won by Erl King and Provider respectively. Although some Eagle-Eyed people were quick to snap up the 2-1 offered about Erl King, especially as he won at 4-5.

Tuesday March 30th was a typical dull and uninspiring day's racing. The opening event was the Sherwood Selling H'cap, for three-year-olds and up over 6 furlongs. The race was won by the Moylan ridden Byrnhead, who was bought in for 135 guineas. Domilius was left at the start and consequently took no part. Going through the formbook of the time, it was quite a common occurance for horses to be either slowly away or left at the start. So the problems of the 1993 Grand National and it's starter had to face were nothing compared to times of old, when even five furlong races were started by tape.

Confusion reigned for the Bentick Plate over 1 mile 4 furlongs. When Laggard who was a recent winner at Lincoln & Liverpool and his jockey Dick expected to ride him.However the trainer Loates, took the decision not to run, even though the horse was in the racecourse stables.

It was not a race, on which you could get rich though, because the winner was the 20-75 favourite Crowned Head. His jockey Cooper must have most definately fancied the horse's chance, even before the withdrawl of Laggard. For he ran twice around the course so as he could go to scale at 7 stone 2lbs.

The Wilford Selling Plate caused little interest as a race. For it was won without any diffuculty by the Vic Tabor trained Knight of York, as his owner had to go to 260 gns to keep him. But two runners were sold as the Bonanza filly went to Mr Edge for 34 guineas, while a Mr Clowes bought Mowat for 20 giuneas.

The connections of Blue Danube forsook his engagement in the last race on the card, so as they could concentrate on the days big race, the Newark Handicap worth £262 over the straight mile. Punters no doubt took the hint as he was a well backed 3-1 second favourite, the end result being that he was beaten a quarter of a mile out.

Epsom Trainer Vic Tabor Had Many Winners At Midland Tracks Including Knight Of York At Colwick

The market leader Talana Hill at 5-2, did not fair much better though finishing third, beaten a neck and 1½ lengths. Sir Artegal ridden by R.Stokes, just managed to hold the late rally of Dunholm with Thwaites up. However it could have easily been a different result for Dunholm was left at the start and lost several lengths. Incidentally Dunholm was owned by Lord Durham, whose younger brother was The Honourable George Lambton of 'Hyperion' , and 'Men and Horses I Have Known Fame.'

The five furlong Bestwood Park Handicap went to Mix up, who only the previous season raced seventeen times without success. Trained by Sam Darling who was an even bigger martinent than his younger brother Fred. It was reckoned that the victory was due entirely to the riding of Wing, who completed a double for the two day meeting.

Mr H.H.Collins (Owner of Blue Danube) received some compensation. When his two-year-old filly was an easy two length winner of the five furlong Robin Hood Plate. In fact she was that impressive that, that days Nottingham Evening Post reported:- "Taking them altogether, they were a useful lokking lot, and the winner will require some catching.

Yet again punters lost their money when the 9-2 second favourite Odde whipped round, and was left at the start.

Of the seven race card, six of those were flat races. The last one was the Oxton Hurdle Handicap, which did not go by without incident. As the leader in the 2 mile race, Kirkgate decided to jump the rails instead of the second last. So leaving the 9-4 favourite Catch Penny, ridden by Georges Parfrement, to win by three lengths. Catch Penny was owned by popular Nottingham steward Colonel R.L.Birkin.

Parfrement had the distinction of being the only Frenchman to win the Grand National as a jockey. This he did in 1909 on Monsieur James Hennessy's Luttuer III. Parfrement also won the

Grand Steeplechase de Paris three times. After all his glories acheived on the racecourse, he finally met his death, due to a fall from Field Marshall at Enghien in 1923.

The original intention was to hold National Hunt meetings, in the month of December 1914 and February 1915. But due to the aforementioned military encampments at Colwick Park, this was not at all possible.

A record number of entries had been attained for both meetings. However the National Hunt committee took the decision to allot Nottingham a two day meeting on April 12th & 13th 1915.

The meetings opening race was the Trent Selling Hurdle, which saw the return of a great perenial in Vic Tabor's Wild Aster, who was made favourite at 6-4. Wild Aster was one of the characters of the equine world and was still going strong as a fourteen-year-old. But that was nothing compared to his eighteenth year, when he made racing history, in to say the least, what were unusual circumstances.

In 1919 Wild Aster won three races in the space of a week as an 18 year old. One of only five of that age to win a race. The roll started at Wolverhampton on 4 March when dead-heating for a selling hurdle. Four days later he finished second in another selling hurdle, this at Haydock.. But was given the race as the jockey on the first past the post had been warned off. The treble was completed at Warwick on 10 March, when after dead-heating for a third selling hurdle, he won the spoils outright as the jockey on the other horse dismounted in the wrong place.

Returning back to the Nottingham race of April 12th 1915 he finished fifth. His jockey happened to be Ernie Piggott three times Grand National winning rider on Jerry M 1912, Poethlyn in 1918 and 1919. He later went onto become grandfather to the legendary Lester. The winner was Horatio Bottomley's Bouton Rouge, there being no bid.

You can guarantee that if this horse was at all fancied by connections he would not have gone unbacked. For Horatio Bottomley was one of those colourful characters, whose attraction to "The Sport of Kings", was due to the betting side,.A one time member of parliament who was later sent down for a seven year stretch in 1922 for fraud.

He won over £50,000 when Northern Farmer landed the Stewards Cup at Goodwood in 1899. While Wargrave won the 1902 Ebor and the Cesarewitch two years later. For all his successess he died pennyless in 1933. Best remembered now for the reply he gave in a court case, for when asked "you keep racehorses Mr Bottommley?".He answered "No they keep me".

Of the six runners that started for the Elvaston Handicap Steeplechase. It was reduced by a third, at the first fence, when both Shotwell and Dick Dunn refused. The race went to Fleeting Peace ridden by Georges Parfrement.

The third race on the card, proved to be a very bad race for punters and must have had them screaming of "fix". Only four went to post for the 2 mile Newark Selling Handicap Chase and there was just the one finisher, that being the 6-1 outsider to boot. All seemed to be going well until halfway when the leader Flying Louis market leader at 11-10 ran out and took the 9-4 second favourite Joey M. The next fence saw the demise of Roman who. was on offer at 4-1, to leave Coton in the hands of Mr. Harry Brown, to come home alone. Not surprising after such a catalogue of errors, there was no bid for the winner.

Harry Brown was everyone's idea of what an amateur jockey is. Leading gentlemen over sticks in the period 1918-21. He was also overall Champion Jockey in 1919 with 48 winners, the last amateur to be champion jockey. Charlie Peppercorn was based on him in 'Memoirs of a Foxhunting Man'. While never winning the Grand National or Cheltenham Gold Cup, he was second in both races. Like his elder brother Frank, he possessed great charm and wit. So much so that Harry was racing advisor to the Prince of Wales later Edward VIII. Both Harry and Frank eventually turned to training with mixed fortunes.

The Harrington Handicap Hurdle saw the return of Catch Penny, favourite at 3-1, who had a strong chance of defying his 12 stone 8lbs when he fell at the last, along with 7-2 second favourite Macmerr. The two length winner was Silverian ridden by Dale, after making all the running. This race along with the previous one (a seller) were the richest on the card at £96. Even accounting for it being war time, it was a meagre return,

An Edwardian Post Card Of Wild Thing Winning At Nottingham. The Main Stand Survived Until It Burnt Down In 1986

Wetherby trainer George Gunter rode his charge Tittleby to a three length victory, in the two mile Annesley Hurdle. Gunter was the type of trainer, who invariably knew what time of day it was. This being one instance, as Tittleby was a well backed 7-2 chance.

The final race of the day saw Mr Harry Brown complete a double, in the three mile Hunters Handicap Chase. It was a case of equine experience over youth. As the winner was Sir Abercorn a 13 year old, while the runer up was Gale II at a year younger. The other runners were a six year old and two sevens, one of which Emperor V broke down.

The Nottingham Evening Post of April 13th 1915 described that days racing as "delightful weather favoured the concluding stage of the Nottingham April Meeting, and the sport was again interesting, albeit fields were of moderate proportions."

Jockey William Payne, who had not been long back on leave, rode his first winner since joining up, on Rosslare the 6-5 favourite in the Clifton Selling Chase. There being no bid for the winner. Apparently he would have ridden at Colwall, the day before, but his licence did not come through in time. Champion N.H. jockey in 1911 with a then record 76 winners. After he retired from riding, he trained Blaris the winner of the Innaugural Champion Hurdle (1927). While on the flat his biggest success was in the 1949 King's Stand Stakes at Royal Ascot, in so doing beating Abernant, the highest rated sprinter since World War II.

A Lord Lonsdale success was always popular with the paying public, and Mark Minor's win in the Colwick Handicap Hurdle was no exception, especially as he started an 11-8 favourite. It also being the first leg of a treble for Georges Parfrement.

He was generally called "The Yellow Earl", due to the suit's he wore, the very livery of his servants and the colour of his Rolls Royce's. Although he had few big wins on the racecourse, his one Classic success, being with Royal Lancer in the St Leger of 1922. He was universally liked, the one exception being King Edward VII. Lonsdale was once described as "almost an Emperor, but not quite a gentleman".

The days third race was the 2 mile Rufford Selling Handicap Hurdle, in which there was only three runners. The pace was pedestrian until the last hurdle when the market leader Gulvain set sail from home and, mamaged to hold on by a short head, from Carol Singer. The winner was owned and trained by G.A.Butchers while his son G.F.Butchers, was the rider. At the subsequent auction he was knocked down to the owner of the second, Mr J.Baylis for 80 guineas.

Colonel Birkin's Queen Imaal made all the running to win the £96 Nottinghamshire Handicap Chase over 3 miles. The 11-10 favourite had Georges Parfrement up, while eight lengths back in second place was Fermoy ridden by the aforementioned Mr Frank Brown.

Lord Lonsdale completed a double and George Pafrement a treble, when King Connor a 6-1 chance, ran out a length winner of the 23/4 mile Gonaldstone Handicap Hurdle. All of Georges Pafrement's three winners were trained by Whitaker, at Royston.

Willie Stephenson trained there in the 1950's &60's. From where he sent out triple Champion Hurdler Sir Ken 1952-54, Grand National winner Oxo 1959. While his biggest win was with Artic Prince in the 1951 Derby.

Comfort landed his sixth consecutive victory in the 2 mile Tollerton Handicap Chase. The 6-1 third favourite, of five, won by two lengths . The win completed a first and last race double for William Payne and his trainer father R. Payne.

Due to the demands of a war torn Britain then it was to be almost four years to the day, before Horse Racing returned to Colwick Park.

Chapter Seven

After the Great War

Monday 14th April 1919, was D.Day, as far as Colwick Park was concerned. For a mixture of fine sunny weather and it being, the only race meeting all week, saw a bumper turnout. Unfortunately it was not the case on the equine front as only 23 horses ran at the meeting.

Action got under way, with the five furlong Colwick Selling Race, worth £100. The winner being Mr W de Pledge's All Clear ridden by A. Rhodes and trained by his father J. Rhodes. The three year old colt was sold to Lord George Dundas for 310 guineas. The second was Curie who was claimed by J. Rhodes for 160 guineas. While the race itself may have been uneventful, the start certainly wasn't. For the tapes were broken three times, before the starter managed to get them away.

You could say that Lord George Dundas followed in the footsteps of the Hon. George Lambton. For at the time it was unthinkable for a member of the nobility to enter any profession, even training racehorses. While he did not have the success that Lambton attained to, Dundas still managed to make a fair living out of it. Amongst the winners he sent out were, Pomme de Terre (owned by his father the, 1st Marquis of Zethend) in the 1920 Manchester November Handicap, as well as Yutoi in the Cesarewitch of 1921. His greatest sadness was that, he outlived Hurst Park racecourse, for as chairman he was very much against it's closure in 1962. A much loved course, at the side of the Thames, it fell prey to property developers, while the turf was dug up, and re-laid at Ascot to make their National Hunt track.

Lord George Dundas Sent Out Many Runners At Colwick From His Hill Cottage Yard At Newmarket.

The day's second event was the one mile (run on the round course) Trent Selling Plate of £100. Which went to the 5-2 on favourite Towyn apparently he was not all that genuine, as he had run the occasional dodgy race. But he still managed to win by five lengths in the hands of Victor Smyth. The winner was subsequently bought by a Mr Brueton for 80 Guineas.

The jockey's victories on the flat included, Brownhylda in the Oaks and the Ascot Gold Cup with Happy Man both in 1923. While he also won the Cambridgeshire of 1916 on Eos. Later turning to training, he became something of a hurdles specialist, winning the Champion Hurdle four times, with Seneca (1941), Forestation (1942) which he also owned. But the best horse he trained was National Spirit who won in 1947 and 1948.

Favourite backers got their fingers burnt when the 1-3 Sunny Moya, was beaten in the five furlong Little John Plate for two year olds. The concession of seven pounds to Prince Herod proved too much, who ran out a one and a half length winner. The jockey being George Hulme. Whose major wins included the Ascot Gold Cup of 1919 on By Jingo, he also won the 1924 2,000 guineas on Diophor. He was only 35 when he died in Hungary in 1934 during a stomach operation, having moved there five years earlier to ride for his subsequent father-in-law Herbert Reeves.

There was a very disappointing turnout for the day's big race, The Nottingham Spring Handicap. Only four went to the post for the mile and a quarter race. Significant support saw Roi Hero, who carried bottom weight of 8stone 8lbs, return the even money favourite. His backers were not to be disappointed, for he ran out an easy four length winner.

Vic Smyth completed a double when King Sol the 7-2 on favourite, was an eight length winner of the Rufford Abbey Handicap.

The one mile 3 furlong Clifton Plate went to Roker who landed the odds of 2-1 by 1 length from Double Chance.

Roker was ridden to victory, by possibly the greatest horseman of the twentieth century, Steve Donoghue. Ten times Champion Jockey, winner of six Derby's including two war time Derby's at Newmarket. He is also the only jockey to ride three successive Derby winners 1921-23 Steve as he was affectionately known, had the gentlest pair of hands to grab hold of a rein, while he rarely used the whip. Never once did he fall foul of the stewards, but you could never say the same about the owners he rode for. As he invariably broke contracts and riding arrangements, especially come Derby time.

Double Chance, The horse back in second never set the flat racing world alight, but six years later it was an entirely different matter, for he won the Grand National. At the time of his Aintree victory his, part owner and trainer Fred Archer, a nephew of the leading 19th century jockey.

Double Chance as well as Roi Hero was by Roi Herode, whose best son was The Tetrarch. The spotted wonder as he was known was nothing short of a phenomenon. Unbeaten in all his seven races. He only ran as a two year old and many noted judges consider him to be the fastest horse ever to grace the English Turf.

The Nottingham Evening Post for Tuesday 15th April 1919, for that day's racing read:- " in the expectation of witnessing rather better sport than was provided yesterday another large company assembled at Colwick Park this afternoon, and there is no doubt that as racing gets back to the normal the Nottingham fixtures will again be amongst the most popular in the Midlands".

The day's opening race was the five furlong Wilford Selling Plate, which went to Mr.A.Barton's Ambassador ridden by Cooper, who won easily by a length. The winner must have created a big impression for the owner had to go to 410 Guineas to retain her. The two year old filly's success provided a good idea to the ability of the progeny of Ambassador. For it was the first time any of his progeny had been on a race course.

Finishing last but not least in the eight runner field, was Lord Jersey's Musk Deer, with Fred Templeman up. Templeman had just recently returned from India, and Musk Deer was his first mount of the season. Later that year, he went onto ride Lord Glaney's Grand Parade to victory in the Derby. While as a trainer, he sent out Chatelaine to win the 1933 Oaks, and the 2,000 Guineas of 1930/41 with Diolite & Lambert Simnel respectively.

There had been some exceptionally close betting in the Sherwood Selling Handicap over six furlongs. The exchanges concerned Lanorf at 6-5 favourite and Simon's Craft a 6-4 chance.

But it was not so tight in the race, for the favourite finished last of the four runners. Which left Simon's Craft ridden by H.Allsop to fight out the finish with Happy Maid. Victory going to the former by a head. At the subsequent auction the winner left the ownership of Mr G.Egerton and joined Major Weyland, for 340 Guineas.

After the meagre turnout for the first day back, things took a decidedly turn for the better on the second day of the meeting. For apart from the opening race of eight (double the previous day's best). Eleven went to post for the five furlong Robin Hood Plate, for two year olds. To say that it was an eventful race would be something of an understatement, all of which the 5-2 on favourite Parella avoided.

Even before the off Olton's Beauty got loose at the start and bolted four furlongs down the course. Then turning round he headed back and ended up at the mile start, where he stayed while the others got under way. But there was still more excitement to come, for both Treasury and Royal Sign collided as the barrier went up, causing Treasury to unseat his jockey.

All of which, as mentione left the favourite was unaffected. He took up the running at halfway to win by two lengths, in the hands of Clark. People were sufficiently impressed to describe it as a "stylish performance"

The £262 Newark Handicap over one mile, turned out to be something of a benefit for the bookmakers. The winner being the 20-1 outsider of five, Speen, in the hands of a certain Keith

Piggott riding only his second winner, having ridden his first at Newbury the previous Friday. Although able to do 6 stone 9lb for the ride, it was not to be long before he was having trouble with his weight and consequently he had to turn to "The Winter Game" for rides. Where he gained major successes on African Sister in the 1939 Champion Hurdle and the 1925 Welsh Grand National Vault both trained by his uncle Charles. Later to training, he became the Champion Trainer for the 1962-63 seasonlargeley as a result of winning Grand National with Ayala.

Favourite at 2-1 was Rich Gift who finished next to last. Owned by Lady Torrington, she was more than just a good friend of the horse's jockey Steve Donaghue. One place behind the favourite was Athletic, who the day before had finished second to Roi Hero in the Nottingham Spring Handicap.

By the way, the horse that finished second to Keith Piggott's mount, was Tunworth ridden by a jockey called Lester, now there's a coincidence for you.

The victory of Miss Maid in the £100 Bestwood Park Handicap over five furlongs, was to be significant in the career of Tommy Weston. The reason being that the jockey on the beaten favourite Steve Donaghue was that impressed, by the 16 year old Tommy Weston that he introduced him to the trainer Alfred Sadler who was looking for a young lad to ride Arion in the Kempton Park Jubilee Handicap, which that year (1919) was run at Hurst Park. After he won the Jubilee Handicap by six lengths, one thing gradually led to another, as trainers became to recognise his talents in the saddle.

The end result being that Lord Derby gave him a retainer at the beginning of 1924 to ride the Stanley House Horses. By 1926 Weston became Champion Jockey. As well as riding the winners of eleven classics, including Hyperion who won the 1933 Derby and St Leger. However he has gone on record as saying that Sansivino the 1924 Derby winner was the best that he rode.

For 1919 there were three further meetings planned, each comprising two days. Those being the 7/8 July, 11/12 August and the 6/7 October. However the October meeting had to be abandoned due to a rail strike at the time.

National Hunt Racing had to wait, right until the end of the year, before it returned to Colwick Park. Yet again it was a two-day meeting. Monday 1st December being the date and it was a case of nothing special to write home about. In fact the most notable point of the day's racing was the weather. For little could be seen of the racing due to thick fog.

The Castle Selling Hurdle saw the joining together of two sports. For the winner Hukm was owned by World Billiards Champion Melbourne Inman. Starting favourite at 4-9 he led all the way in the hands of Davies to win by 30 lengths. There was no attempt made to retain him, so consequently he was sold, to a Mr.E.S.Tomlinson for 175 Guineas.

Mr. G. Sankey was described as an enthusiast supporter of National Hunt racing and his George B had no trouble at all, in landing the Trent Selling Handicap Chase over two miles. Ridden by Hehir he won by two lengths at odds of 2-5. While there was no price quoted about his only opponent Warbine. The winner was subsequently sold at the auction for 220 Guineas to Mr W Lea.

It would be reasonable to assume that quite a few punters got their fingers burned, over the defeat of Ullswater in the two mile Bentinck Handicap Hurdle. Having been backed down 5-4 favourite, on the basis that he was well clear on the book, his well being was also justified for he was a recent winner at Leicester. Added to this he had travelled up from Lewes near Brighton and was ridden by Ernie Piggott.

But all of this was to be of no avail. As punters saw their money go west, for Ullswater finished third beaten a length and two lengths. The race proved to be a benefit to the Brown's for the winner Appleton, was trained and ridden by Harry Brown. While the six year-old chestnut Entire was owned by his wife.

Just three runners turned out for the three mile Mapperley Handicap Chase. However the race did not lack excitement. For a close finish was witnessed between the 5-4 favourite Llangollen and the complete outsider Jack Symons, who was on offer at 5-1, victory going to Jack Symons by a short head, who also had the distinction of being the oldest in the field at 14, the other two, were 9 year olds Three lengths third was Shunbally who started at 5-4. The winner was owned by war hero Colonel G. Paynter, while the trainer and rider was Frank Lyall. Like his four brothers Frank Lyall rode with some success over fences, the best of them being Bob. Frank finished second on Bloodstone in the 1912 Grand National.

There were joint favourite's for the three year old Clifton Hurdle over one mile 4 furlongs, in Eothen and Cuban at 6-4. Such a race would be unheard of nowadays, but right up until the late 1950's, three year old hurdle's over one a half miles were commonplace. Although by January 1st of each jumps season the juvenile hurdler's had to race over two miles.

Going back to the Nottingham event, both the favourite's, had to settle for minor honour's, for victory went to Sam Temple ridden by T.Hulme, an 8-1 chance.

The victory of Sandy Cuba, in the day's closing event, the Elvaston Chase over two miles, provided jockey T.Hulme, with the day's only double. Even though, there were only five starters, the race was not devoid of calamities. For at the first fence Branton Queen fell, then the second favourite Hairpin II went some way out. While Viva who happened to be leading at the last fell, which left Sandy Cuba the 6-4 favourite, to win by a distance from Victor Haig.

The Nottingham Evening Post of Tuesday December 2nd 1919 reported that days racing as thus'

'The difference from the miserable of yesterday at Nottingham to those in evidence this afternoon was remarkable. Instead of a raw cold temperature and fog, the latter of which obscured all view of the running, there were glimpses of sunshine and a perfect light. What is more, the arrivals list, to the surprise of many, proved greater than anticipated, and thus ensued a marked improvement in the sport.'

Simon's Craft arrived for the opening race the Selling Three Year Old Hurdle, of which, he would have undoubtedly started favourite. But at the last moment his owner Mr Edge, took the decision to withdraw him.

The honour of Market Leader fell to Rozy Picton who started at 4-5. However she found one too good for her, in the shape of Mr.C.Ford's Mundelo, ridden by his trainer Mr Casebourne, who was subsequently sold at the auction, to the owner of the second Mr.A.Long.

As you have no doubt gathered by now, it was the norm, to have seller's as the first two races on the card and December 2nd 1919, was no different from any other, for it saw the imaginatively named Colwick Selling Handicap Hurdle, mind you I must admit there was a bit more thought gone into it, than the naming of the previous race.

The day's second race, was over two miles, which saw the defeat of another odds-on favourite, in Gamelyn at 4-5. This time victory trainer Mr.T.Lund, and ridden to a five length victory by Milburne.

Landteel was a prolific winner, as well as having a great following with the public. Whose money forced him down to 4-5 favourite for the Welbeck Handicap Hurdle over two miles six furlongs. However the price did not matter to his owner Mr.H.Beckett, for he had little or no interest in betting, as all he wanted to do was to win as many races as possible. He was not

Page 111

to be disappointed for Landteel in the hands of J.Payne ran out a five length winner from the Cuban. Cuban was going one better, than the day before, for he finished third in the Clifton Hurdle.

Punters latched onto the chances of the Irish raider King's Carol, in the day's big race, the two mile Midland Handicap Chase worth £233. In what was the best race of the day, he went down by just a neck to Straight Ahead ridden by T.Hulme.

The two mile Broughton Hurdle saw the biggest field of the day, in which twenty took part. Prep started 6-4 favourite only to fall three hurdles from home victory duly going to the 20-1 outsider Sherwood Forrester ridden by his trainer Mr Casebourne. In so doing he was completing a double.

Odds-on backers went home happy, for Top Hole who started at 2-5, led all the way to win the Ruddington Chase over three miles. The winning jockey was William Payne, no relation to the J.Payne who won earlier in the afternoon.

That prolific writer of the turf J.Fairfax-Blakeborough (in that he wrote over 100 books on racing). He also happened at some time or other a owner, assistant trainer, amateur rider, Clerk of the Course, judge, starter, you name it he did it. In 1927 he had his much acclaimed The Analysis of the Turf published by Philip Allan and Co. Ltd. In it Fairfax-Blakeborough tells of a story from sometime in the early 1920's:-
"I remember once being amused at Nottingham by seeing a jockey coming out of the weighing room only to be immediately surrounded by waiting information seekers who attacked him

from front back and both flanks "Can I speak to you for a second? said the first to reach him.

"Not if it's anything about racing or subscription lists", he replied in a tone that was definite".

Chapter Eight

Golden Miller, Sir Geordon Richards
and the Wragg Brothers

Many consider the 1930's to be the golden age of racing. Top Jockeys like Sir Gordon Richards, Harry Wragg, Tommy Weston, Charlie Smirke and Freddie Fox all rode at the top of their form. Equine stars included Golden Miller, Brown Jack and Hyperion.

Golden Miller undoubtly the most famous steeplechaser before Arkle and Red Rum had very early connections with Colwick Park. As Arkle never raced here, Golden Miller is without a shadow of a doubt the greatest chaser ever to appear at Colwick . He won the 2 mile Annesley Hurdle on January 26th 1931. Ridden by Ted Leader, he anticipated the start only to get caught in the tapes and lose a tooth. All this did not stop him landing the odds of 5-6. Still then in the ownership of local owner and sportsman Philip Carr, whose son Arthur played cricket for Nottinghamshire and captained England. The family connection with racing is maintained through a mile and three quarters handicap named in Arthur Carr's honour, which is run at Nottingham's Monday evening meeting in late July.

Ten months later "The Miller" passed into the ownership of Miss Dorothy Paget, more of whom later, on the advice of the horse's then trainer Basil Briscoe. With the immortal words "I have the best chaser in the world", Golden Miller and the best hurdler in England, Insurance. Subsequent events proved that he was not far wrong for The Miller won five consecutive Cheltenham

Gold Cups 1932-36, and the 1934 Grand National, in so doing he became the only horse to win racing's two premier chases in the same season. While Insurance became the first dual winner of the Champion Hurdle (1932 and 1933).

Dorothy Paget; Fell Out With The Nottingham Executive After Celebrating At The Course

During the 1933 flat season Gordon Richard, later Sir, was carrying all before him and by the end of the year he had set a new seasonal record total of 247 winners. At Nottingham on October 3rd of that year "Moppy" as he was affectionately known won the last race on the card by one and a half lengths. The mount being Barnby a 3 year old carrying 7 stone 13lbs, in the five furlong. Elvaston Handicap. Although that was nothing special it was over the next two days that he proceeded to make racing history. For at Chepstow, Gordon rode eleven consecutive winners. With his Nottingham victory that made a world record of twelve.

Horse racing more than any other sport, has families within its community. One such family was the Wragg brothers each of whom rode with success during the 1920's , 30's and 40's. There being Arthur, Harry and Sam, the most successful of which was

Harry. Who won the Derby three times on Felstead (1928),

Golden Miller In Action

Blenheim (1930) and a wartime substitute at Newmarket with Watling (1942). While he was Champion Jockey in 1941 with 71 winners. Universally considered to be the most intelligent of riders of his time. He was given the nickname of "The Head Waiter", due to his tendency for leaving it until the last possible moment before swooping through to get up on the line. While he undoubtedly lost races he should have won, his mounts hardly knew they had a race. While it was a complete rarity for him to win by as much as a length.

In 1947 he turned to training and he popularised the method of timing horses on the gallops. His highlight being winning the 1961 Derby with Psiduim. The tradition has been continued by his son Geoff who won the 1983 Derby with Teenoso.

So at Nottingham on the 26th March 1934, the Wragg brothers did a 1-2-3. For in the Rufford Abbey Handicap over 6 furlongs, Arthur won on Tetraset a ten year old carrying 8 stone 9lb. Second was Biretta a four year old with 8 stone 8lb ridden by Sam. While Harry the eldest of the brothers three finished third on the four year old Hillsbrow carrying 8 stone 6lbs. With ten runners in the field, it was not exactly a foregone conclusion that they would fill the first three places, especially as both Tetraset and Hillsbrow started at 9-1.

Not many people could claim to have been struck by lightning and survived. Yet a story related to me by Mrs Taylor wife of former Head Groundsman Phil Taylor, about his predecessor

Jack Marshall. That one day in the mid 1930's (no exact date can be ascertained) he was on the far side of the course, when a bolt of lightning struck him on the shoulder. For quite a while he was laid out cold, with his faithful dog at his side. Eventually help reached him, but he had a whacking great big scar on his back to show for it.

Everyone I've spoke to, who remembers Jack Marshall speak of him with great affection and respect. While at the same time they say he was not the sort of man you would want to cross swords with, in that what he said was law and that was the end of the matter. Another story told me , this time by Harry Holmes who for many years did the building work at the course, best illustrates the standing he held. The tale involves another formidable character of the turf the redoubtable Miss Dorothy Paget. The trouble arose over her often gargantuan appetite. In that sometime in the late 1940's (unfortunately yet again the date cannot be verified) she kept the racecourse restaurant busy late into the night, of which they were paid handsomely. However as far as Jack Marshall was concerned this was definitely not on, for he liked everyone to have left by 7.30 so as he could lock up. As they were way past this time, he decided to go up to her entourage and ask them to leave, after a heated argument everyone upped and left. Dorothy Paget though was not the sort of person to let something like that go by without mention. For she wrote a letter of complaint to the racecourse committee, their reply to her was that in future would she mind not holding her parties, if that is the right word for such a retiring person. Her reply to that was that she would never set foot on Nottingham Racecourse again.

Dorothy Paget was one of the few owners who was bigger than the sport itself, in more ways than one. Generous to a fault to those she felt deserved it. She demanded extreme loyalty from her employees, which she returned in kind . To best illustrate the effect she had on racing an extract is reproduced from The Winter Kings by Ivor Herbert & Patricia Smyly published by Pelham Books / Stephen Greene Press (1989):-

She broke with many trainers and jockeys and moved her string in sudden swoops around the country in some quarters she was regarded with awe, in others with near terror. But those who knew her best and served her longest spoke of her with a warmth transcending loyalty, Charlie Rogers (her Irish stud Manager) said "she was a wonderful person. When I was ill she sent flowers and the food I liked best and had me flown to Ireland and back. She sent me 99 word Christmas telegrams. She thought a lot of Gordon Richards", Rogers recalled "She was a good judge of people and liked those who were straight. She was 100 per cent straight herself". So much so that her bookmakers knowing she usually slept by day, let her back horses in the evening after they had run, trusting her absolutely not to have found out the results.

Sir Gordon (Richards) who rode for her on and off for nearly 30 years and then trained for her for six more recalled: "one heard a lot of stories about her messing her trainers about, but that never happened to me. She left everything absolutely in my hands. I never want a better owner and she was the best loser I have ever known. If any of the boys got hurt while riding her horses and had to go to hospital, there were always parcels for them".

"Frenchie" Nicholson who was the last of her many English jumping trainers thought her a "marvellous owner, one of the best".

Nottingham Evening Post 1941: Note The Headline Of 'Huge Colwick Attendance'

When she died this eccentric part-recluse, half-terryfying, half-terrified person had won 1,534 races. No one has yet come along to fill the gap this vivid creature left.

Chapter Nine
A Darkness Descends

If you look at the list of racecourses closed since 1900, a very large number closed there turnstiles forever at the outbreak of the second world war,. Racing was savagely cut back but in consultation with the government the jockey club allocated a limited number of fixtures as it was decided to keep some racing going as a morale booster. Nottingham was given the honour of hosting the 1940 Cambridgeshire, Jockey Club Cup, Cheveley Park Stakes and Middle Park Stakes.

That great autumn handicap carried the prefix New along with the three other transfers from Newmarket.The Cambridgeshire was run on November 2nd and was the first Saturday meeting at the track for 37 years, it was also the first time a running commentary was used at Colwick Park. It was the first time the Cambridgeshire had been run on a Saturday. Prior to that it had always been run on a Wednesday.

Dorothy Paget had four entries for the New Cambridgeshire, which was run over the straight course. Of those entries one was the five year old Colonel Payne, who the previous season had been heavily backed for Royal Ascot's Cork and Orrery Stakes. Most of the money wagered originating from the horse's owner. Her first bet was known to be £10,000 and by the time they were off her total outlay on the race was anybody's guess. All on the strength of the speed he has shown on the gallop's, which had convinced trainer Fred Darling (who was not averse to having a bet himself) that he was a certainty. Having started at 11-10 on Colonel Payne ran like a drain, and as you can guess Miss Paget was not best pleased. As the horses jockey no lesser rider than Gordon Richards was unsaddling, she inquired as to where Fred Darling was of which he gave the immortal reply:- *I wouldn't be quite sure, Miss Paget but I've a pretty shrewd idea he's on top of the stand cutting his throat. From that day until the day she died they were the firmest of friend.*

Fred Darling

Colonel Payne was scratched and did not run in the New Cambridgeshire, and the only one of Miss Pagets entries to run was the Walter Nightingale trained Sister Carol, which finished nowhere. The winner being Major Rigg's Caxton at 100-7 trained by Fred Armstrong and ridden by Percy Evans. It was a 1-2 for outsiders, as in second place was the 100-6 shot Mr Ramsden's Heavy Weight, beaten half a length. While a neck back in third was the 100-30 favourite, Mrs Bendir's Quarter Maitre. Quarter Maitre had incidentally already won that season's Lincoln. He also had the distinction of running in the name of the wife of Arthur Bendir, he just happened to be the then owner of Ladbrokes. Admittedly though they were not the force that they are today.

The New Cheveley Park Stakes was an uneventful race to say the least, which went to Mr Peter Beatty's Rosette Filly. As already mentioned horse's were then allowed to run unnamed as two year old's and she was subsequently given the name of Keystone. Having started at 13-8 on, she ran out an easy five length winner. It was yet another victory for one of racing's most enduring and successful partnership's: Fred Darling and Gordon Richards.

Different to Richards in temperament, in that at his best he was hard and unanswering, while at his worse he was ruthless either with horses, stable staff, owners or journalists. But their attention to detail and dedication was nothing less than 100%. While anybody who worked for Fred Darling had nothing but respect and admiration for him. His record speaks for itself, six times champion trainer, he also won flat racing's premier race The Derby, seven times. In addition he bred Gordon Richards only Derby winning ride Pinza (1953)

Aldershot	last meeting 1 April, 1939	Hooton Park	last meeting 26 December, 1914
Alexandra Park	last meeting 8 September, 1970	Hurst Park	last meeting 10 October, 1962
Birmingham	last meeting 21 June, 1965 (evening meeting)	Keele Park	last meeting 12 May, 1906
		Lanark	last meeting 18 October, 1977
Blackpool (Clifton Park)	first meeting 1 August, 1911; last meeting 26 April, 1915	Lewes	last meeting 14 September, 1964
		Lincoln	last meeting 21 May, 1964
Bogside	last meeting 10 April, 1965	Maiden Erlegh	last meeting 12 April, 1906
Bournemouth	first meeting 17 April, 1925; last meeting 10 April, 1928	Malton	last meeting 4 February, 1904
		Manchester	last meeting 9 November, 1963
Bridgnorth	last meeting 20 May, 1939	Monmouth	last meeting 4 May, 1933
Bridgwater	last meeting 13 May, 1904	Newport	last meeting 17 May, 1948
Buckfastleigh	last meeting 27 August, 1960	Northampton	last meeting 31 March, 1904
Bungay	last meeting 29 May, 1939	Oswestry	last meeting 29 April, 1939
Burgh-by-Sands	last meeting 16 April, 1900	Paisley	last meeting 10 August, 1906
Cardiff	last meeting 27 April, 1939	Pershore	last meeting 1 May, 1939
Carmarthen	last meeting 17 April, 1914	Picton	first meeting 19 April, 1909; last meeting 11 April, 1914
Champion Lodge (Maldon)	last meeting 29 April, 1903		
		Plymouth	last meeting 5 September, 1929
Chelmsford	last meeting 29 April, 1935	Portsmouth Park	last meeting 13 April, 1914
Colchester	last meeting 4 April, 1904	Ross-on-Wye	last meeting 18 April, 1904
Colwell Park	last meeting 25 May, 1939	Rothbury	last meeting 10 April, 1965
Cottenham	last meeting 7 May, 1925	Sheffield	last meeting 5 November, 1901
Croxton Park	last meeting 2 April, 1914	Shincliffe	last meeting 6 May, 1914
Dawlish	last meeting 20 September, 1900	Shirley Park	last meeting 11 March, 1940
Derby	last meeting 9 August, 1939	Stockton	last meeting 16 June, 1981
Dunbar	last meeting 22 March, 1906	Tarporley	last meeting 26 April, 1939
Gatwick	last NH meeting 28 March, 1940; last Bona Fide meeting: Old Surrey & Burstow meeting 24 April, 1948	Tenby	last meeting 29 October, 1936
		Torquay	last meeting 25 March, 1940
		Totnes	last meeting 1 September, 1938
Harpenden	last meeting 7 May, 1914	Wenlock	last meeting 5 May, 1939
Hawthorn Hill	last meeting 4 April, 1939 (re-opened after the last war as a Pony Turf Club track)	Woore	last meeting 1 June, 1963
		Wye	last meeting 2 May, 1974
Hethersett	first meeting 16 April, 1903; last meeting 4 May, 1939		

List Of Courses Closed since 1900

The day's other big two year-old race The New Middle Park Stakes, went to the 10-1 shot Hyacinthus owned by Mr A.Basset and trained by Henry "Atty" Persse whose best horse was easily The Tetrarch. While the winning rider was Patrick Beasley of the famous Beasley clan and was often referred to as Rufus.

The country's stayers were put through their paces in the two and a half mile New Jockey Club Stakes, which saw the 5-2 favourite Atout Maitre run out a four length winner. Owned and trained by Herbert Blagrave, with Charlie Elliot up . A horseman of the highest calibre, confidence was not one thing he lacked. Having won the Derby three times, he remains the last apprentice to have been flat jockey's champion, in 1923 and 24.

The day was such a success that the Nottingham Evening Post of November 2nd 1940 reported thus:- "To-day's programme was the most ambitious ever staged at Colwick Park, and all the enclosures were well filled. The chief event was the New Cambridgeshire Stakes, for which a representative field went to the post. Probably the biggest crowd since the boom years of 1918-19 saw the Cambridgeshire decided for the first time in it's history away from Newmarket.

After the mammoth crowd for the New Cambridgeshire meeting, all attendance records were broken for their Easter Monday meeting on April 14th, 1941, when over 41,000 people turned up. There is no chance now whatsoever of that figure ever being exceeded.

With the war and it's restriction's gradually beginning to bite into the British way of life, it was inevitable that a number of racecourses would be taken over for military purposes. Nottingham proved to be no exception to this. But as the bumper turnout for the Saturday October 11 meeting of 1941 showed, folk still loved the chance of forgetting about the rigours of war for an hour or two. this also happened to be Colwick Park's last flat meeting of the duration.

Proceedings got under way with the five furlong Byron Plate Handicap for three-year-olds. The race was heaven sent for punters, as it went to the 4-1 favourite Sugar Palm, who carried top weight of 9stone 7lb to a half length victory. Trained by Frank Hartigan his biggest successes being the 1915 1,000 Guineas and the Grand National of 1930 with Shaun Gollin. The winning rider was Tommy Carey who before 1941 you would as likely have seen riding at Northolt Park and Hawthorn Hill. As he was the leading jockey in the field of Pony Racing in which he won the Pony Derby on more than one occasion at Northolt. His biggest win in conventional racing was the 1943 Derby (run at Newmarket) for Dorothy Paget, on Straight Deal.

Early Light who led from the start was reckoned to be an unlikely loser. For just after halfway he swerved across the course, while at the finish he was beaten a total of 1a quarter lengths into third place.

The imaginatively named two year old Maiden Plate over five furlongs went to Organza the 5-2 favourite, by two lengths. Ridden by Dick Perryman, who won the 1,000 Guineas three times as a jockey. While as a trainer he gained immediate post-war recognition by saddling Charnossaire to win the 1945 St Leger, and the Derby, St Leger double in 1946 with Airborne.

The winning trainer was Walter Earl, who holds the distinction of having been private handler for two of racing's leading owner / breeders in Solly Joel and the 17th Earl of Derby. For whom he sent out Watling Street to win the 1942 Derby.

Favourite backers were out of luck in the five furlong Highfields Handicap for the race went to the 8-1 shot Zaitor, with Eph Smith, the Eph incidentally stood for Ephrain. He had a long and distinguished career as a jockey, which included the 1939 2,000 Guineas and Derby on Blue Peter. Who more than likely would have won that seasons St Leger but for the intervention of the war, which caused the cancellation of the race. In 1954 he won the King George V1, Queen Elizabeth Stakes on the Queen's Aureole.

Zaitor was sent out by Belguim born Henri Jellis, whose biggest success as a trainer was with Happy Knight in the 1946 2,000 Guineas. While as a jockey he won the 1927 St Leger with Book Law and the Oaks of 1929 and 35 with Pennycomequick and quashed respectively.

It proved to be a tight one for the judge for the first three past the post Zaitor, Love's Revelry and Azam Pasha, were each separated by a head. How much easier it is for them now with the photo finish camera.

There was yet another tight finish, this time for the seven furlong Sherwood Nursery, which saw Courtly ridden by K.Mullins and trained by P.Whitaker win by a neck, at odds of 10-1. The battle for second place was between those two Smith brothers Doug and Eph. The verdict going to the younger Doug on High Table by a neck from Eph on Wedding March. Doug was five times champion jockey and was a great rider of stayers winning the Ascot Gold Cup twice, Doncaster Gold Cup Cesarewitch and Jockey Club Cup each six times. But the best horse he rode was undoubtedly Petite Etoide to win the 1,000 Guineas of 1959. Like a lot of great jockeys when they turn from riding to training they fail to fulfil expectations, although Doug Smith did win the 1969 Oaks with Sleeping Partner. Twenty years later, he was found dead having committed suicide whilst suffering from acute depression.

Favourite backers got back into their stride, with the victory of Coolnargeat at 7-2, in the one mile Autumn Handicap for three year olds. Ridden by Dave Dick and trained by George Todd. Both men were masters of their craft as well as being approachable to boot.

Dave Dick is so far the only man to have ridden winners of both legs of the Spring Double. Having won the Lincoln as a 17 year old in 1941, he had to wait fifteen years before completing the double. When in 1956 he won probably the most talked about National of all on E.S.B.. For when jumping the last Queen Mother's Devon Loch looked assured of immortality. That was until up that long Aintree run-in fate decreed otherwise, as Devon Loch by and land the spoils.

George Todd was a trainer of infinite skill, who had to wait until the twilight of his career to collect his only Classic success with Sodium in the 1966 St Leger.

The naming of the one and a half mile Forest Plate H'cap, must have brought back a few memories for the old timers, of racing on the old course. The race went to the Michael Beary ridden Buxton the 2-1 favourite by two lengths. Beary was given the nickname of "The Stormy Petrel of The Turf", for he had a temper to match. Winner of four Classics including the 1937 Derby on Midday Sun. While as a trainer he won the 1951 2.000 Guineas with Ki Ming, only to fall into financial trouble. Buxton was trained by the Honourable George Lambton.

A point of interest on this race, there were two horses that had very similar names. Those being the five-year-old Romeoll ridden by Dave Dick and Rodeoll a nine-year-old with Cliff Richards up (younger brother of Gordon). So it was a case of punters watch your bets, however neither of them troubled the judge. For the nearest either of them got was Romeoll who finished fourth.

The day ended with the one and a quarter mile Paddock Maiden Plate. Which went to the three-year-old The Derby Star a 10-1 outsider ridden by P.Maher to a one length success. Trained by Fred Butler, while he did not attain the heights acquired by his elder brother Frank. He still added his name to the Epsom roll of honour by sending out Mid Day Sun to win the 1937 Derby.

It would be another four and a half years before Flat Racing returned to Nottingham. However it was not the end of wartime racing at Colwick Park, for there was a National Hunt meeting on Saturday December 20th 1941.

Both Gerry Wilson and Ron Smyth each rode doubles. The latter kicked off matters with a six length win on Kentucky, in the juvenile Hurdle over one and a half miles. Kentucky who was an American bred, was generally held to be the leading juvenile hurdler of his generation. Little of what there was of the season. He was originally owned by Sir Malcolm McAlpine. But after his first victory of the season at Worcester, he was subsequently sold to Mr.C.Blunt who also trained him from his stables at Letcombe Regis Wantage. So it was little surprise that he started at 6-5 on.

Ron Smyth ended the season as Champion N/H Jockey with twelve winners. A situation that caused his father to comment caustically:- "That he must be the best of a bad lot".

For the two mile Bingham H'cap Chase, it was a case of Brothers-in-law to the fore. As it was a one-two for Gerry Wilson and Fred Rimell. Tweeldee II the 9-2 favourite carried Gerry Wilson to a three length victory over the Fred Rimell ridden Knight o' London.

The winner was trained by Reg Hobbs and owned by Mrs Marion du Pont Scott. A partnership that gained it's biggest success with the victory of Battleship in the 1938 Grand National. The winning jockey on that occasion was Reg Hobbs son Bruce who became at seventeen the youngest winning rider. As well as being the owner of a Grand National winner Mrs du Pont Scott was also married to Hollywood star Randolph Scott.

While Gerry Wilson will always be remembered for his association with Golden Miller. On whom he won the 1935 Grand National and the Cheltenham Gold Cups of 1934 and 35.

The two mile Mansfield H'cap Hurdle went to the 11-4 favourite Steel Blade ridden by Ron Smyth and trained by his father H.E.Ram. Along with Gerry Wilson up finished second.

Chasing débutante Broken Promise won the Novices Chase over two miles. Starting at 10-1 he won unchallenged, having led all the way. Of the 22 runners, 12 fell, most of which was due to the winner's fast and accurate jumping.

Broken Promise was ridden by M.Prendergast and trained by F.Horris. While his owner Mr James Rank was a genuine enthusiast. Easily the best horse he owned was Prince Regent the 1946 Cheltenham Gold Cup winner.

You might say that the victory of Schubert was music to the ears of punters. Starting a 4-1 joint second favourite he won the three mile Nottingham H'cap Chase by four lengths. The success of Schubert completed a double for the then reigning champion. N/H jockey Gerry Wilson. The trainer was C.Beechener. In second place was Luxborough ridden by Herbert "Frenchie" Nicholson, whose biggest win came on MedocII in the 1942 Cheltenham Gold Cup. As well as being the father of David "The Duke"

Nicholson, he also for many years ran a successful jockeys academy. The most famous prodigy being Pat Eddery.

The victory of Southport in the two mile Beeston Maiden Hurdle, continued the long successful association of a certain L.Piggot's ancestors with Nottingham. For he was ridden by Fred Rickaby, Lester's cousin. Starting a 9-4 favourite he ran out an easy three length winner, so at least the punters went home happy. Fred Rickaby later emigrated to South Africa, where he made his name as a trainer.

Southport was trained by Dudley Williams, whose biggest win albeit as a jockey came with Kellsboro Jack in the Grand National of 1933.

So came to an end National Hunt racing at Nottingham during World War II. Although there were meetings planned for January 17,31 and February 28 1942, but they had to be abandoned because of the war.

However by early 1942 the National Hunt Committee were coming under extreme pressure to put an end to wartime jump racing. They decided that the 1941-42 season would be the last for the foreseeable future. The obvious honour falling to both Cheltenham and Wetherby, the former holding the Gold Cup on Saturday 21st March. The last race being at Wetherby by eighteen minutes.

National Hunt made it's return at Cheltenham on Saturday 6th January 1945. Although there was racing planned for both

Wetherby and Windsor on Boxing Day of 44. For Nottingham it was to be another thirteen months before the course was to see The Sport of Kings again.

Chapter Ten
The Immediate Post War Years

With the end of hostilities in 1945, life could gradually start returning back to normal. However in the meantime, many a racecourse had fallen by the wayside in that six year period. Fortunately Nottingham survived, but the first meeting after the war was nearly a shambles.

"Hundreds of people at the station going back" said a "doggy looking punter". "Half the course is under water." put in another. "We shall get drenched if it keeps like this", said a third. "We're drenched already" replied the first man. "All right, we're drenched, and the track is under water and everybody's gone home" said the first man wearily," so let the horses get drenched an all. That's what I say".

Even due to the inclement weather, racegoers were not to be deterred. For apparently Colwick Road (which at the time was the only route to the course from the City Centre and still the major one) was jam-packed with cars by about 1o'clock.

Mind you the Racecourse Management could undoubtedly have organised things better. For punters were further inconvenienced by a lost set of keys. As A paragraph taken yet again from the Nottingham Evening Post describes the situation at hand thus:-

"A bunch of keys that had become mislaid caused hundreds of racegoers to stand in the pouring rain waiting for admission to the enclosures, when queues began to form more than an hour and a half before the first race became due. Officials searched high and low for the missing keys, and tried several bundles without avail. About one o'clock the turnstiles clicked and the soaked patrons quickly made their way to the refreshment rooms".

I would imagine it to be a reasonable assumption that at was impossible for them to pass on the views of the irate racegoers for the Post prides itself on being a family paper.

Despite rumours which had been circulating to the effect that water had to be pumped off the course. As well as there being considerable doubt about racing taking place both proved incorrect, and racegoers were not to be disappointed. For the two day meeting was of the highest quality, which saw the winners of four champion hurdles and a Gold Cup, even though only one of them was to land the spoils.

Fred Rimell is one of only two men (the other being Fred Winter) to be champion as a jockey and trainer under National Hunt rules. But it was as the trainer of four Grand National winners that he gained everlasting fame.

So it's to Fred Rimell that goes the honour of riding the first winner at Nottingham for over four years. In which his mount Palermo won the two mile Annesley Maiden Hurdle Division by one and a half lengths, at 7-2 success was kept in the family, for the winner was trained by Fred's father Tom, who sent out Forbra to win the 1932 Grand National. Palermo was following hot on the heels of a victory at Wincanton and was only able to run in the Nottingham event because it was a maiden at closing race.

George's Beeby and Archibald who provided the runner-up Treasury in Division 1 went one better in Division 2 of the Annesley Maiden Hurdle, with Cardy. He was a recent import from Ireland and was an easy three length winner at 8-1. George Beeby twice won the Cheltenham Gold Cup, they being Brendan's Cottage (1939) and Silver Fame (1951). While his son Harry was one of the founders of the Doncaster Bloodstock Sales.

The Old Racecourse Station Closed In 1959

The Colwick Handicap Hurdle over two miles must have been a race to truly savour. For taking part was the reigning Champion Hurdler Brains Trust carrying 12 stone 4lb. But the best he could do was third, beaten a total of thirteen lengths. While the winner carried three pounds more was Distel, who next time out was to win hurdling's premier race. Apart from winning consecutive Champion Hurdles, Brains Trust and Distel did have one other thing in common. For the latter was owned by Miss Dorothy Paget while the former was bred by her, but sold after his three-year-old season.

Distel was trained in Ireland by Charlie Rodgers and ridden for the first time by Robert Ryan, who also had the ride in the Champion. Favourite was Diver at 5-2, who was a more than useful hurdler who carried 12-6, but was beaten five lengths into second.

Dorothy Paget and Charlie Rodgers landed a quick double, when Verbatim the evens favourite won the two mile Newark Handicap Selling Chase, subsequently sold at the auction for 550 Guineas to Major Neville Crump. Which must have been a rarity indeed, for it was the exception rather than the rule for one of Miss Paget's horses to be sold after winning a seller. The jockey was Dan Moore who in 1975 was to make racing history by sending out L'Escargot to win the Grand National. In so doing he became only the second horse ever, to win the Cheltenham Gold Cup (1970&71) and Grand National, the other being Golden Miller.

The four length victory of the 9-4 second favourite Unconditional Surrender, in the two mile Mansfield Handicap Chase, was nothing spectacular. Although it did provide the second leg of a double for the Rimell family.

It is interesting to note that the third horse the twelve-year-old Phychic Bid, ran in the Bingham Handicap Chase at Nottingham's previous meeting over four years earlier, where he fell. On both occasions he was ridden by George Archibald.

Six of the days seven races were over two miles, the one exception being the three mile Wollaton Chase, which went to the 6-4 favourite Gormanstown ridden by D.Doyle. Jockeys great and small owe a big debt of thanks to the winning owner and trainer Mr Clifford Nicholson, he was one of the founder members of the Injured Jockey's Fund. The best horse he owned was undoubtedly the 1956 champion hurdler Doorknocker whose stable-lad was no lesser person than the now leading flat trainer Jack Berry.

The day ended with Division 3 of the Annesley Maiden Hurdle, which provided the third leg of a treble for Dorothy Paget, with the 7-4 second favourite Sun Storm. But this time trained at Epsom by Walter Nightingale and ridden by Dan Moore. Ten lengths back in second was the 4-5 favourite Fordham.

The second day back, was in complete contrast to the meetings opening day. For where there was torrential rain, there was brilliant sunshine.

Epsom carried on the good work, initiated by Sun Storm in the last race of the previous day. For the Rufford Handicap Hurdle over two miles, went to the Vic Smyth trained Reel, ridden by his nephew Ron. Starting a 7-2 second favourite he just managed to get the better of the 8-11 Market Leader Master, by one and a half lengths.

If the first day results were as bleak as the weather for the bookmakers. The second day saw a decided turnaround in fortunes.

Even for allowing Goyanna's recent Wetherby success (for which he incurred a 7lb penalty) he was still allowed to start at 20-1, for the 2 mile 6 furlong Stayer's Handicap Hurdle. It is fair to assume that the main reason for this being, that he was trained by the relatively new H.Hitching and not that many racegoers would have heard of him. He made all the running, in the hands of Pringle to win easily by eight lengths.

As if that was not bad enough for the punters, there was more of the same to come. For Division 1 of the two mile Carlton Handicap Hurdle, went to the 20-1 outsider Little Pip, ridden by E.Hannigan. While he was owner trained by a T.W.Jones.

Things did not improve, when the 100-6 chance Brightner Sandy, with J.Smith up won the 3 a half mile Nottinghamshire Handicap Chase, by four lengths. Incidentally as it was worth £294, it was the most valuable race of the meeting. He was trained at Tadcaster by William Arthur Hall, but was known to one and all as Charlie. He has a race named in memory of him at Wetherby's second October meeting.

Beaten a total of seven lengths into third place, came a 13-year-old carrying 11 stone 9lb. The horse in question was the 1940 Cheltenham Gold Cup winner Roman Hackle, of which he was one of Dorothy Paget's record seven winners of chasings Blue Ribband.

One of the most stylish jockeys of the post-war period was Bryan Marshall, and he brought home Coronation Laddie by ten lengths, in Division 1 of the two mile Elvaston Chase. Yet again another outsider, he was owner trained by Clifford Nicholson.

Marshall was Champion Jockey in 1947-48 season, as well as winning the Grand National's of 1953 and 54, with Early Mist and Royal Tan respectively.

Division 2 of the two mile Elvaston Chase, saw a horse of great personality, character and ability, although at the time racegoers could have had no inkling whatsoever. His name was National Spirit and he was to lift hurdle racing to undreamed of heights. He went onto win the Champion Hurdles of 1947 and 48. In the first one he beat the subsequent Prix'd'l'Arc de Triomphe winner Le Pallion.

However in this race he hardly distinguished himself for he ran out, when ridden by his regular partner Ron Smyth. It did give a brief respite though to favourite backers for it went to Paradise Club who won by four lengths at 2-1, in the hands of a jockey by the name of Ruttle. It proved to be yet another success for George Beeby.

The day began with a two mile Handicap Hurdle and also ended with one, in the Carlton Handicap Hurdle Division 2. Which went to the appropriately named Victory, who managed to scrape home by a short head at adds of 10-1. He was ridden by his trainer, who was someone called Street.

With virtually unraceable conditions, even for jump racing on National Hunt's return at Nottingham. The ground was the complete opposite for flat racing, with it being firm on the first day, and even hard on the second.

For April 22nd 1946, apart from it holding the distinction of being Colwick Park's first flat meeting for four and a half years. It also had the added attraction of it being Easter Monday. A bumper crowd was to be expected and the course executive were not to be disappointed. A report in that day's Nottingham Evening Post best exemplified the size of the crowd:-

The Silver Ring and Tattersalls enclosures had been specially enlarged to cope with the numbers expected, and when the runners for the first race were at the post, racegoers were still arriving in large numbers.

Two specials from the Nottingham L.N.E.R. station were well patronised but a large fleet of buses bore the brunt of the traffic. Although a special shuttle service operated between the city and course it was inadequate to meet all demands and many people made the journey on foot.

From 12.30 onwards a long stream of vehicles bumper to bumper, stretched along Colwick Road from the course almost to the city. A large force of police were on duty all along the route, and they kept the traffic moving slowly although from the vicinity of Meadow Lane onwards it was quicker to make the journey on foot.

The number of private cars was comparable with pre-war standards, and although there were large areas of parking space, the accommodation was taxed to the utmost. Many drivers left their vehicles in streets within a short distance of the course.

So many people were intent on seeing the opening day's programme that getting to the course presented a problem in itself, and there were some amazing traffic scenes. Some indication that there would be a large crowd came from the unusual influx of people from outlying districts on the early trains. From daybreak onwards the police dealt with many inquiries as to the best way reaching the course, but it was at noon that the rush really started.

The paper goes on to say:-

Colwick Woods also housed a crowd, for it was possible to watch the racing from this unofficial "grandstand" free of charge.

Even after the first race, thousands of latecomers were pouring into the course, and the city there was a crowd over 50-yards long still waiting for buses after the 2.30 race had been run.

So the scene was set fair, and what a day racegoers were about to witness. The riding honours entirely belonged to Joe Sime claiming 5lbs, one of the most popular of all post-war jockeys. He endeared himself to Nottingham patrons by riding the first three winners and only a neck separated from victory in the fourth.

His day got under way with a five length victory on the 6-1 shot Child of Dawn. She was making her racecourse debut in the five furlong Fillies Maiden Plate for two-year-olds. While the 6-4 favourite La Pompadour lost her chance by swerving across the field at the start.

Child Of Dawn was trained at Newmarket by Jack Waugh, Jack was won of a large racing family and something of an Ascot specialist. He eventually retired in 1970 and succeded by Sir Mark Prescott.

The 1941 Cambridgeshire winner Rue De La Pait, landed the one mile Trent Selling Handicap . Although in between he had changed hands, for his Cambridgeshire success he was owned by Mr Leonard Abelson, who was later to achieve everlasting success with National Spirit. Rue De La Pait was bought by Mrs Swannand and trained by Mr Beechemer. The even money favourite had to be bought in for 310 Gns. Rue De La Pait was the only horse to win at Nottingham before and after the war.

At the time of his four length Nottingham Rue De La Pait was owned by a Mrs S.W.Swannand trained by a Mr Beechener, at even money. He was later bought in for 310 guineas.

Joe Sime completed his treble, and Jack Waugh a double with the half length victory of Kirkdale, in the seven furlong Rufford Abbey Handicap.

Even though Joe Sime was on the crest of a wave, he just failed to land the one mile three furlong Nottingham Spring Handicap. The £690 prize went to the J.Simpson ridden, Henri Jelliss trained Unitas. Starting a 7-4 favourite, he had a neck to spare over Joe Sime on Auralia. Indeed this must have been a difficult race for the judge. for a head back in third was Frankie Durr claiming five pounds on Scarlet Emperor. Aphrodice finished a neck behind in fourth, while the fifth was Sussex Martlett, who was only half a length off. The last of the six runners was Ponte Tresa, who was three lengths out the back.

Only three went to the post for the two-tear-old, Little John Plate over five furlongs. Which went without trouble to the 11-10 favourite Wingard ridden by F.Wadsworth. The win provided one of the few successes for his owner trainer Pat Donaghue, whose father Steve was one of the greatest jockeys of the 20th century.

The trainer, jockey partnership of Henri Jellis and J.Simpson took the day's last race with Bottleneck. The judge had yet another close decision, for the Clumber Stakes over one mile two furlongs went to the 3-1 chance Bottleneck by a short head, over the 11-8 favourite Mubarak. While a further short head back in third was Trump Card.

To end the report on this historic and chaotic day, there was a reply on the traffic conditions in the following day's Post thus:-

Mr.H.Morley, deputy manager of the Nottingham Transport Department, told the "*post*" today, that the fact of any in conveying the public, to the races yesterday, was not due to any shortage of vehicles, but to the congestion on the route caused by the tremendous number of motor cars and other conveyances.

"We began operations at 10.45am". he stated *"and had made ample provision for later developments, but the line of traffic was so dense that very often cars and buses were crawling along almost touching each other".*

That brings us onto the second day of the meeting Tuesday April 23rd 1946. The opening race went to Tipstaff. Although he had not managed a win in the last eleven starts, he still went off a 4-6 favourite. Ridden to a two length victory by Cliff Richards younger brother of Gordon. His sole classic success came in the 1945 2,000 Guineas with Court Martial. The winning trainer being yet another member of the Waugh clan, this time it was Alec.

The market for the two-year-old Wilford Selling Plate over five furlongs, suggested that it was a two horse race, and that is exactly how it turned out. For it saw the 5-4 favourite First Jacqueline ridden by Arthur Wragg suffer a length defeat at the hands of the 11-8 second favourite Player. The winning trainer owner being Ernest Davey, while the jockey was Ken Gethin. The latter went onto have a very successful association, with most popular of post-war handicappers Operatic Society.

In the Bestwood Park Maiden Plate over five furlongs, the betting yet again told the whole story. For they went Deemster, 2-1, Golden Rule 9-4 and Swamp Fire 3-1, and they finished exactly in that order. Deemster was ridden to a five length victory by Peter Maher, while he was trained at Malton by Hollowell. It was a lot closer for second place though, and the judge must certainly have had his work cut out. For a head and three neck's separated the next five home.

The County Handicap, over the straight mile saw a closely fought finish, between Charlie Elloit on Eric's Folly and the Michael Beary ridden Glide Away. With Elliot's mount who was a 6-1 chance just landing the spoils by half a length.

It proved to be another success for one of racing's great families. This time it was the Watt's. For John Evelyn Watts won the 1927 Derby with Call Boy, he also sent out Corrida to win the 1936&37 Prix de l'Arc de Triomphe's. He is also the grandfather of the present day Richmond trainer Bill Watts.

The trainer jockey partnership of Ernest Davey and Ken Gethin, landed a double with Hazel Bridge, in the five furlong Robin Hood Maiden Plate for three-year-olds. Starting at 100-7 she won by three lengths.

The Bentick's (the family name of the Duke's of Portland), have a long association with racing at Nottingham. So it was that the first flat meeting back after the second world war, came to a close with the one and a half mile Bentick Stakes. A race that no doubt sent a few punters home happy for it went to the 11-10 on favourite St Clement ridden by Gordon Richards. While his trainer Major Sneyd is best remembered in teaching three fine jockeys, in the Smith Brothers Eph and Doug, and the supreme stylist Joe Mercer.

Just after 9.00 on the morning of Thursday January 16th 1958, two vampire training aircraft from R.A.F. Swinderby collided. Although the crash happened in mid-air over Colwick, it was visible from all of Nottingham, even as far off as Bulwell, which is a good 6-7 miles from Colwick.

The four airmen involved were killed, one who was found near Colwick Hall. Also killed was a Mrs Mona Ellen Collis, by falling debris.

Wreckage was scattered over a wide area, including the fuselage of one which landed on the racecourse. At the time it was described as "sticking out like a dart".

There was a variety of witnesses to the accident. One was the wife of the then Head Groundsman Phil Taylor, who lived near the old mile start. A workman came rushing onto the house to tell her of the crash and as she told me *"she ran out just in time to see the planes coming down"*.

Another witness was John Gostall an electrician who was working at the racecourse stables and was quoted in that day's Nottingham Evening Post:- *We were standing in the stable yard" As we were walking from the stables for our breakfast we heard a loud bang. We could see three pieces of wreckage coming down almost on top of us. One of them fell on the racecourse and the other narrowly missed the side of the stables at the back of us. We ran onto the course to see if we could give any assistance. We fancied we could see two shapes which we thought might be the pilots drifting over the edge of Colwick Woods.*

While Fred Bass who was another electrician also working at the stables said *"It was right above us and we were very lucky to escape."*

The 1st May 1961 is a date that has long gone down in the long turbulent history of betting. For it saw the legalised opening of off course betting shops. Nottingham holds the honour , as it was the first live commentary by Extel in a legalised betting shop. . This was the 5 furlong East Leake plate for two year olds, which went to the Eph. Smith. ridden Black Nanny. He started 2-1 favourite and was owned by Mr Jim Joel.

Chapter Eleven

Closure Threatens

The 1960's was not just a black decade for the railway's. For it was also a dismal time for British Racecourses. As it saw the demise of Buckfastleigh, Hurst Park, Woore , Lewes, Lincoln, Manchester , Birmingham, Bogside and Rothbury

That illustrious list, very nearly had another casualty added to it. For as the Guardian Journal of the 10th July, 1965, reported that racing at Nottingham might come to an end.

Four months later a national politician was dragged into the debate. For the then Minister for Sport Mr. Denis Howell, spoke at some length on the positive side of keeping a racecourse in Nottingham.

As reported in the Guardian Journal of 2nd November 1965, on the speech given the previous day by the said M.P.at the inaugural meeting of the East Midlands Regional Sports Council:-

He said at a press conference that Colwick Park was one of five major projects he had pinpointed as being open to aid from the council.

Later he said *"I have had discussions with the local authority, and have told them my views. But the final decision rests with them"*.

He said he hoped Colwick Park would be used for other sporting activities, between race meetings.

Asked about financial help from the Government for the development of the park by Nottingham Corporation. Mr Howell said *"Special levy boards are set up for this purpose, and they are not my pigeon"*.

He said the racecourse was one of five major projects in the East Midlands region with exciting possibilities.

Only the previous month, Alderman Eric Foster had told a meeting of the City Council Development Committee that the possibility of keeping Colwick Park for racing for another three years was being looked into.

At a City Council meeting on 8th November 1965, the decision was made to hold racing at Colwick Park for the next two year's.

NOTTINGHAM Racecourse Company shareholders have approved the sale of Colwick Park to Nottingham Corporation for £500,000 — a figure agreed at last month's meeting of the City Council.

The chairman, Col. R. T. Thompson, gave three main reasons for the sale.
● Falling attendances at mid-week racing.
● Increased costs.
● Little prospect of increasing profits over the present level.
Racing will continue as scheduled until the end of 1965, the last meeting being the National Hunt fixture on November 22. There has been racing on the Nottingham course since 1892.
Shareholders voted 21-7 in favour of the sale.
Mr. E. W. Mugglestone, the company's consultant surveyor said that initially the Corporation offered much less money and when the offer rose to £500,000 the company was told that it was the limit or the Corporation was no longer interested.

Had the company waited for a more favourable time to sell, present Government legislation would have meant a lower price.
The site would have been valued on its present use at £120,000 and this would have been raised by one-third to £180,000.
Asked about the gravel deposits, Mr. Mugglestone said that 14 years ago there were negotiations with the Hoveringham Gravel Co. but these collapsed when planning permission was refused. It was unlikely that anyone other than the Corporation would ever be able to extract the gravel.

Col. Thompson said the company was likely to exist for some time to come and liquidation was not immediately foreseen.

The racecourse is situated in Colwick Park, which consists of 293 acres and includes the historic Colwick Hall.

Nottingham will be the second Midland racecourse to close down this year, Birmingham having ceased after their meeting on June 21.

City Council Meeting Reported in The Guardian Journal On The 8th November 1965.

One of the reasons why the City Council did not use Colwick Park for housing was that the water table is less than two feet below the ground. Although saying that the course drains very well, and racing is rarely abondoned due to waterlogging.

One significant alteration made after the takeover, is that there is no longer a straight mile. For the first two furlongs had houses built on it, as well as a pub logically called The Starting Gate.

On the 9th of August 1965 Colwick Park received a Royal visit from Prince William of Gloucester. Sadly though it did not have a happy ending for his filly Hypodermic split a pastern in the Byron Handicap Plate and had to be destroyed. Victory went to Peter Robinson on Resolved.

RACING was reprieved, officially, last night for the £500,000 Colwick Park racecourse. Nottingham Corporation are to arrange meetings there for at least two years, 1966 and 1967, and will use this breathing space to decide on the long-term future of the valuable site, which they agreed to buy earlier this year.

It is the first time Nottingham City Council have entered the racing business, but they are not the first authority to do so—Doncaster and Brighton, among others, beat them to the post.

Three City Council committees took the decision last night. Ald. Eric Foster, chairman, said members of the General Purposes, Finance, and Development Committees had gone into all the pros and cons before coming to their conclusion.

No cash help

Their attempts to obtain financial support from the Turf Board, the Levy Board or the Minister of Sport have failed.

"There will be no financial help from them, although they are all very concerned about the future of the racecourse," said Ald. Foster.

Visiting the district last week, the Minister of Sport, Mr. Dennis Howell, indicated that he thought the continuation of racing essential for Colwick Park. He has twice met the Town Clerk (Mr. T. J. Owen) for talks on the project.

Four named

Four members of the City Council were appointed last night to go fully into the business of organising racing. They are Ald. Foster, Ald. W. G. E. Dyer, Ald. L. Mitson and Coun. O. S. Watkinson.

"A very early meeting will be called of this sub-committee to confer with the officers of the present racecourse company," said Ald. Foster.

The Corporation hope to engage two of the racecourse officials to run the meetings, and the Town Clerk will be legal adviser.

In racing circles last night the Corporation's decision was widely welcomed, but there was reluctance to comment until further details have been worked out.

Newspaper Article About The Council Getting Involved In Racing For The First time

The Ford family more than any other has been associated with racing in Nottingham. In many ways it was like a dynasty for it passed on from father to son. But all that came to an end on February 2nd 1967, for it saw the retirement of Mr Francis.S.Ford. His replacement was who many regard as the greatest of all Clerk of the Courses in John Hughes. For through his tireless hard work coupled with boundless enthusiasm, he helped to save both Aintree and Lingfield courses.

It is often said that 3 runner races are unexciting especially when there's no betting interest. But on November 16th 1971, this could not have been further from the truth. For it saw the 2 ¾ mile Colwick Cup Chase. The field was headed by a true immortal in Crisp who was trained by a man of no lesser distinction in Fred Winter. The other two runners being Domingo and Scotch Reel who each received a stone.

The race as the betting suggested was no contest (actually there was no betting). For Domingo unseated his rider at the first and remounted, but it would have made absolutely no difference at all for Crisp won by 15 lengths with the same distance between Scotch Reel and Domingo. Less than eighteen months later galloped into turf history, by just failing to lead all the way in the Grand National, when getting caught on the line by Red Rum.

Chapter Twelve
From Stan Mellor to Lester Piggott

When people talk of Nottingham Racecourse they usually speak of two record breaking jockeys. One being the inestimable Lester Piggott of whom we shall hear more of later. While the other is Stan Mellor, who on December 18th 1971 at Colwick Park became the first National Hunt jockey to register 1,000 career wins.

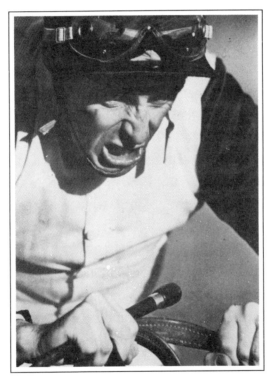

It was an extremely momentous occasion, as well as it being this author's first memory of Nottingham Racecourse, which was mainly due, to the gone but not forgotten I.T.V.7.

For as the Evening Post of that day reported it was a joyous time for everyone in attendance.

Two races later he proceeded to make it 1,001, with victory on the Charlie Hall trained Clear Cut in the two mile Plum Pudding Handicap Chase.

Stan Mellor was three times champion N.H. Jockey(1959/60, 1960/61, 1961/62). Twice winner of Kempton's King George Six chase. Frenchmans Cove (1964) and Titus Oats(1969). While his most famous success came on Stalbridge Colunmist in the Hennessy Cognac Gold Cup(1966), in which he became one of only six horses to defeat the mighty Arkle in a steeplechase.

After retiring at the end of the 1971/72 season Stan Mellor turned to training, His best Horse being the New Zealand bred Royal Mail who finished third to Aldaniti and Spartan Missle in the 1981 Grand National. Having already won the 1980 Whitbread Gold Cup and finishing second in the 1979 Cheltenham Gold Cup.

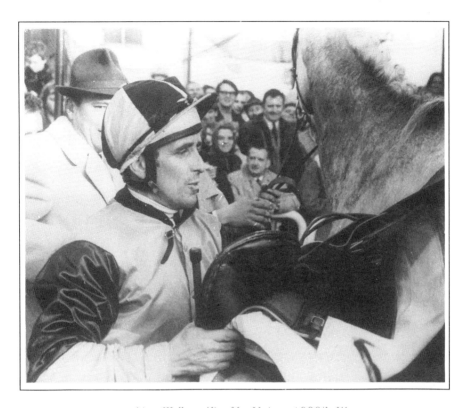

Stan Mellor: After His Historic 1000th Winner

A story related to me by Nottingham racegoer Steve Belton, is of the proverbial one that got away. For at the evening meeting of Monday 24th July 1972, he backed the Joanne Eades ridden Harvest Spider in the Brooke Bond Dividend Cup Ladies Race. And like most of the horse's backers he was counting his winnings, fate decreed otherwise, for the horse's saddle was slipping and she was dumped onto the Colwick Park turf. While the formbook as always bears cold reading:- led after 3 furlongs veered right 2 furlongs out 2 lengths clear unseated rider near post.

Many racegoers thought she had just held on long enough. A stewards enquiry said they had parted company just short of the post. The race went to Tom Rating.

Nottingham helped to make history by hosting the first ever race in Britain for men and women jockeys (in modern times). When on April 1st 1974 in the Ladbrokes Lad's and Lasses Handicap over one mile 2 furlongs. Linda Goodwill on Pee-Mai led a 1-2-3 for the fairer sex, with a two length victory. In second came Sicely Stevens, while Jackie Thorne finished third.

On April 2nd 1977, Red Rum made front page news around the world by becoming the first horse to win three Grand Nationals. By which time he had already put in three appearances at Nottingham. The first of those being in the three-year-old Merit Hurdle over two miles, on November 18th 1968. Where ridden by John Cook he finished third.

His next visit to Colwick Park came on April 15th 1969. In which the four-year-old Bradmore Handicap Hurdle over two miles, provided "Rummy" with his second victory under National Hunt Rules. His first coming at Wetherby eight days earlier. On both occasions he was ridden by Paddy Broderick, one of the true Iron men of the sport. Red Rum's third and final outing at Nottingham came on March 21st 1972, in the two mile six furlong Trent Handicap Chase. Ridden by Macer Gifford he finished third.

Although Silver Buck won two King George VI chases at Kempton 1979 and 80, as well as the 1982 Cheltenham Gold Cup, he was never given the full credit he deserved. No doubt due to the style of his victories which were were never spectacular and rarely more than a length. Of the 34 races he won, one was a walk over and that came at Nottingham on December 10th, 1979 in the Last Chance Chase over two miles six furlongs. When he was ridden by his then regular jockey Tommy Carmody.

Following hot on the heels of Silver Buck came another Dickinson star, Wayward Lad. The Nottingham patron's had a chance to see him on December 15th 1979 in the two mile six furlong, Philip Cornes Novices Hurdle Qualifier. Starting an 11-10 on favourite he won in the hands of Kevin Whyte.

On Saturday 4th July, 1981 Paul Cook rode a treble nothing earth shattering about that you might say. But the difference here was that each winner was ridden at a different course.

His day started at Sandown in the 2.15 with victory on Princes Gate. He followed this up less than three hours later in the 5.00 at Bath by driving home Rocmannolie. Then came a dash across country, to complete his historic treble, in the Notts. Country Football Club Handicap for 3 year-olds over six furlongs at 7.50. Mind you it was a close run thing, for his mount Pavilion the 5-2 favourite scraped home by a neck.

It would be ten years before the treble was completed again (By Gary Carter on Friday 14th June, 1991. At Southwell York and Doncaster).

In 1983 Gaye Brief became the first champion hurdler to be trained by a woman in Mercy Rimell . For his pre - Cheltenham outing he won Nottingham City Trial hurdle on the 19th February, carring 11stone 7 lbs in the hands of Richard Linley.

The 1984 flat season, saw the winners of four of the following year's classics race at Colwick. These being Oh So Sharp who won the 1,000 Guineas, Oaks and St Leger, while Slip Anchor won the Derby. Both were trained at Warren Place Newmarket by Henry Cecil.

For their respective Nottingham successes Oh So Sharp won the Oxton Maiden two-year-old Fillies Stakes by a length and a half on 13th August. While Slip Anchor won the Whatton Manor Stud Stakes, a conditions race over one mile for two-year-olds. The race sponsors being Mr Peter Player, who is also the Chairman of Nottingham Racecourse Company. Slip Anchor was ridden to victory by Paul Eddery on 30th October by four lengths.

The Saturday evening meeting of July 20th 1985 had no earth shattering event or a star to write about. However what it did have was the defeat of not one but two odds-on favourite's that left their backers feeling very sore indeed. These were Choire Mhor at 1-5 and Starlite Nite at 1-10 . Perhaps though punters should have taken the hint, because Steve Cauthen who was going all out to ride 200 winners in a season declined to take the mounts on the so-called Henry Cecil certainties.

Sixteen times, 'Cock of the North', Edward Hide rode his last winner on the 18th May 1986 at Sha Tin, Hong Kong. Though his last British winner was on the evening of Tuesday 13th August 1985. This came in Hi-Tech Leader with a short head victory in the Lambley Handicap over five furlongs. His biggest success came on the Arthur Budgett owned bred and trained Morston in the 1973 Derby.

Lester Piggott On Wind From The Rest, "His Last Ride Before His Retirement". Willie Carson On Gurteen Boy Won.

The date of 29th October 1985 is one day more than any other that is associated with Nottingham Racecourse. For it was then that Lester Piggott rode his "Last British Winner".

Having arrived at the course by helicopter, the Longfellow went straight into a press conference. At which in front of a fair selection of the world's media, he spoke at some length on the life waiting ahead for him. One thing that comes through is his ready sense of one liners. For as Piggott said:-

"It is a sad day, but it comes to everybody. I am looking forward to training. It's been a lifelong ambition of mine, and I'll have about 50 horses to start with".

He later said *"The one thing I am looking forward to tonight, and from now on, is steak and chips. I'll probably have to buy a new pair of trousers in a couple of weeks!".*

Although it was never disclosed how much Piggott was paid to end his riding day's at Nottingham various amounts were bandied about at the time. One guess was £10,000, but no matter how much he cost, the effect was enormous, for an estimated 5,000 people turned up.

The then Clerk of the Course David Henson spoke in enthusiastic raptures on Colwick Park's headlining day. *"This is a great day for Nottingham. It's a scoop really, the whole city seems to be talking about it. I expect at least 5,000. Actually I don't think you will be able to move here today. It's lovely. Lester Piggott retiring at little Colwick Park. Nottingham will be forever on the racing map after this. I have noticed the staff have even perked up this week. The day has given a fillip to the whole place".*

After the press conference he immediately went to the winners enclosure, which he had entered on previous occasions for what he likes best, riding a winner. This time though it was to spend about 20 minutes signing autographs, the majority of them were on special commemorative programmes from the racecourse.

On the six race card he had five rides, the one he missed out on was the first, which was an apprentice race. His first ride of the day came on Gold Derivative in the Bitter End Selling Handicap over five furlongs, although he was to finish nearer last than first.

Next came what all Piggott fans had been waiting for, a winner. This came on the John Dunlop trained 15-8 favourite Full Choke. Who made all the running to win the two and a quarter mile Willimgton Handicap Stakes by three lengths. The cheers he received was more than equal of any of the nine Epsom Derby winners he rode.

Ice Breaker just failed to break through in the Whatton Manor Stud Stake, for he went down by three lengths to the unpronounceable Shtuijeh.

The East Midlands Nursery over one mile 50 yards, saw another great post-war jockey in Joe Mercer on Farig ride his final winner at Nottingham. For less than two weeks later he retired at Doncaster the final day of the flat season. While he never rode a Derby winner and was only once Champion Jockey (1979). Smokin Joe as he was affectionately called did partner an horse in a lifetime, the 1971 2,000 Guineas winner Brigadier Gerard who won 17 out of 18 races. Piggott was unplaced on Amongst The Stars.

His last ride came in the appropriately named Final Handicap over one mile, in which he rode Wind From The West. This time though the gods were not looking favourably upon him, for he encountered trouble in running and was beaten four lengths into second place by the Richard Hannon trained Gurteen Boy.

In between various Piggott memorabilia was auctioned in aid of the Injured Jockeys Fund, including a photo of Lester, signed by all the jockeys riding at Nottingham which raised £720.

Immediately after racing a large crowd gathered around the paddock for a series of presentation's which included a box of his favourite cigars given to him by Lynda Richards, on behalf of the East Midlands Racing Club. While Peter Player owner of Whatton Manor Stud and then a steward at Nottingham, but now Chairman of the racecourse company, presented "The Great Man" with a silver plate!.

Piggott's great friend and confidant Peter O'Sullevan paid his own special compliment. While the Master of Ceremonies Derek Thompson asked The Longfellow *"how he felt after hanging up your boots"*. Lester answered in his own inimitable way *"Great, how do you feel"*.

As he headed towards his waiting helicopter, the crowd suddenly burst into song with *"For He's A Jolly Good Fellow"*.

Of all the messages of good luck he received, it would be reasonable to assume that his most treasured came from no lesser person than the Queen Mother. For Her Majesty Press

Secretary the late Sir Malcolm Gilliat telephoned Colwick Park to say:- ' *On the last occasion that you will be riding in England. I send you my warmest congratulations on your wonderful achievement's since your appearance at Salisbury 37 years ago.*

You have given so much pleasure to so many racegoers here and overseas and you will be sorely missed.'

Lester Piggott more than any other jockey has shall we say his fair share of stories about him. This particular one comes from Henry Cecil's On The Level published by Harrap (1983):- The Season (1969) therefore had ended much more happily than it had begun, (in reference to how poorly it had started and how great it finished. In what was Henry Cecil's first season as a trainer) and had it's funny moments. For most of the time the jockey's championship was closely contested by Lester Piggott and Geoff Lewis, and Lewis looked like establishing a useful advantage from four booked rides at Hamilton Park, two of them on our horses.

Two day's before the meeting Lester phoned to say *"I'll ride your two at Hamilton. Geoff will be at Nottingham"*.

Seeing from the press that Lester was down to ride both my runners, Geoff rung up in a somewhat bemused state to ask what had happened.

"Lester said you would be at Nottingham", I told him.

"But that's a bloody jumping meeting!" expostulated Geoff.

In or out of the saddle, Lester's tactics take a bit of beating.

Lester Piggott

The Front Cover Of the Commerative Racecard For Lesters Last Meeting

Lester On His Final Day

Sixth Race

One mile and 50 yards, for three yrs old and upwards

3.45 THE FINAL HANDICAP STAKES

£1500 added to stakes

Distributed in accordance with Rule 194 (iii)(b) for three yrs old and upwards. Rated 0-35

ONE MILE AND 50 YARDS

£3 to enter £12 extra if declared to run

Lowest weight	7st 7lb
Penalties after October 9th a winner	7lb
Of a race value £500	10lb

JENNINGS THE BOOKMAKERS have generously sponsored this race including a trophy value £200 at the option of the winner.

SS

193 entries 136 at £3 and 52 at £15 Closed October 9th 1985

Owners Prize Money Winner £1436, Second £441, Third £213
(Penalty Value £1866 60)

5 Eliminated under Rule 125

Form	No	Owner / Trainer	Age	st	lb	Draw	
213300	2	**WILD HOPE** Ch g Great Nephew - Grove Star (Upper Case, USA)) Mr B N Hamoud (G A Huffer, Newmarket) ROYAL BLUE, RED sash, BLUE cap, WHITE star.	4	9	9	(8)	M. Miller
40—5035	6	**TIMBER MERCHANT** B g Decent Fellow - Naturally Enough (Approu) Mr T M P Waterman (J R Winter, Newmarket) DARK BLUE and EMERALD GREEN stripes, GREEN sleeves BLUE armlets, striped cap.	4	9	2	(15)	W R Swinburn
130014 BF	7	**WIND FROM THE WEST** B g Creetown - Bonanza (Andrea Mantegna) Mr J J Raphael (P C Haslam, Newmarket) Mr P C Haslam YELLOW, ROYAL BLUE epaulets and sleeves.	4	9	2	(17) in 10lb ex	L Piggott
322500	9	**TOM FORRESTER** C g Absalom - Blak-En-Bloo (Blakeney) Mr Paul Jabet (A J Pitt, Epsom) ROYAL BLUE YELLOW chevron and armlets, YELLOW cap, BLUE spots	4	8	13	(9)	W Carson
411530	11	**SILLITOE** B f Tachypous - Stuff And Nonsense (Crooner) Don Enrico Incisa (Don Enrico Incisa, Caversham) WHITE, LIGHT BLUE and YELLOW striped sleeves, BLUE and YELLOW quartered cap.	3	8	11	(14)	
3400000	16	**THE LODGE PRINCE** B g Pitfer (USA) - Screen Goddess (Caliban) Qualidair Hotels Limited (M J Ryan, Newmarket) WHITE, BLACK diamond.	3	8	8	(1)	
01—5000	17	**DAME DU MOULIN** Ch f Shiny Tenth - Skibouee (BEL) (Boulou) Mr J L Dunlop (J L Dunlop, Arundel) BLACK, MAROON sleeves and hoop on cap.	3	8	8	(2)	

cont'd over

THE FINAL HANDICAP STAKES-cont'd

Form	No	Owner / Trainer	Age	st	lb	Draw	
030—002	19	**FESTIVAL CITY** B g Pitskelly - Persian Silver (Casti And Count age) Mrs J Darnell (Mrs A R Hewitt, Malpas) ROYAL BLUE and RED quartered, YELLOW sleeves BLUE and YELLOW hooped cap.	3	8	8	(5)	W. 'liams
023001	20	**TROOPER SERGEANT** B g Queen's Hussar - Grass Widow (Thatch USA) Mr M J Norman (G A Huffer, Newmarket) Mr G A Huffer LIGHT BLUE, RED star on body and cap, WHITE sleeves.	6	8	7	(20)	
111556	21	**GURTEEN BOY** Ch c Tickled Pink - Joie d'Or (FR) (Kashmir II) Lt-Col J W Deacon (R Hannon, Marlborough) NAVY BLUE, RED chevrons on body GOLD cap.	3	8	7	(4)	A M-Glone
446040	22	**SPITE AND MALICE** B c Hot Grove - La Mirabelle (Prince Hindu) Mr Andreas Sotironiou (M Salaman, Lambourn) ORANGE DARK BLUE diamond, quartered cap.	3	8	6	(7)	F Street
06—0310	23	**PERSHING** Ch g Gunner B - New Way (Narron) Mrs M I Booth (J P Leigh, Gainsborough) YELLOW EMERALD GREEN Cross of Lorraine and cap.	4	8	6	(13)	T Ives
004604	26	**GOLDEN BEAU** B g Crimson Beau - Kantado (Saulingo) Mr D R Nunnett (M F D Morley, Newmarket) DARK BLUE, RED sash and sleeves LIGHT BLUE cap.	3	8	5	(18)	B Rouse
120601	29	**CAROL'S MUSIC** B g Music Boy - Darling Caroline (HOL) (Ilix) Mr Mel Brittain (M Brittain, Warthill) MAROON and YELLOW check, MAROON sleeves, YELLOW cap.	4	8	5	(10) in 7lb ex	K Darey
030000	33	**CHAISE LONGUE** B f Full of Hope - Opera Star (FR) (Appian) Mr J Richards (D L Henley, Lambourn) BLACK and WHITE (halved) horizontally check cap, YELLOW sleeves.	3	8	2	(3)	
00—00	37	**TOMORROW'S WORLD** B g Full of Hope - Friday Brow (Murrayfield) Mrs H J Collins (C P Wildman, Salisbury) PURPLE PINK stars on body BLACK cap, PINK star.	4	8	1	(12)	
0000	40	**INHERIT** Ch c Homing - Royal Descent (FR) (Run The Gantlet USA) Marshall Racing Ltd (W Holden, Newmarket) BLACK, YELLOW epaulets and cap, BLACK spots.	3	8	0	(16)	
350035	42	**A PEAL SUPREME** B f London Bells (CAN) - Above Reproach (Above Suspicion) Mr J J Heffernan (J G Fitzgerald, Malton) MAROON WHITE chevrons, MAROON cap.	3	7	13	(6)	cont'd over

Lester's Last Racecard

Lester Being Led In After His "Last Ride" on Wind From The West

Page 170

Peter O'Sullivan Presenting Lester With Momentoes Of The Day.

Page 171

Of the man himself the record speaks for itself eleven times Champion Jockey. A record 30 classic wins, including a record nine Epsom Derbys.

After his retirement from the saddle he had two seasons of reasonable success of a trainer. Which included a Royal Ascot winner with Cutting Blade in the 1986 Coventry Stakes.

Then in 1987 his world caved in for he was sent to prison for tax evasion. On which he served 18 months of a three year sentence. But more was to come for in October 1990 he astounded everybody by announcing that he was coming out of retirement. And less than two weeks after his comeback he scored one of his most memorable successes on the Vincent O'Brien trained Royal Academy in the Breeders Cup. So the Piggott story continues to roll on.

Chapter Thirteen

From The Ashes The Phoenix Will Rise

On the morning of 23rd March 1986 fate decided that Nottingham would join Chester and Arlington Park Chicago, in that it's grandstand would be ravaged by fire.

The Grandstand after being ravaged by fire March 1986.

The fire was spotted by two policemen in the meadows area of the city at 7.50 a.m. The Divisional Officer of the Fire Service Headquarters was quoted in the Evening Post of 24th March 1986 "that the fire began in the commentators box at the Colwick Park stand. It was unlocked but the door had not been forced. Flames ripped through the high slate and wood roof, burning a hole in the flat roof behind. It was feared at one stage that the whole building might be destroyed.

He went on to say that *"the grandstand front would have to be demolished and part of the third floor of the facilities refurbished. Flames from the spectacular blaze curled under the slate roof 20ft into the air. The blaze could have been started by arsonists or through an electrical fault. We don't yet know the cause"*.

As it turned out it was started by a tramp who burnt some rubbish to keep warm, which subsequently got out of hand.

On the 21st November 1986 it was reported in the Evening Post that *"Nottingham Racecourse £450,000 facelift right on target after the fire which ravaged the grandstand"*.

While the then Clerk of the Course David Henson said:- *"The work is coming along fine. We hope to get finished by the end of March, weather permitting. A temporary covered grandstand has been set up in Tattersalls and racing will continue during rebuilding. It's going to look great"*.

The paper went onto report that :- *Barret vaulted polycarbonate roof covering steel columns will incorporate the commentator's box and side-on camera.*

The finishing line is to be moved. A new judges box and photo-finish accommodation replace the judges tower which is due for demolition.

Grandstand steppings are also being replaced after serious cracks appeared although the original foundations will remain.

The total cost of the project will be almost £450,000 with the contract being awarded to G.F.Tomlinson and Sons Ltd of Derby. Racecourse Technical Services Ltd is providing the judges box (£58,500) and the Horse Race Betting Levy Board is making a grant of £21,000 towards the crush barriers. The remaining costs will be funded by the Racecourse Executive, insurance claims and a Levy Board Loan.

The new grandstand was eventually opened on Easter Monday April 1987 by ex N.H Champion Jockey turned trainerJonjo O'Neill. His riding career will always be associated with two horses Sea Pigeon and Dawn Run. But at the time of the opening he was fighting a battle against cancer, which thankfully he was able to win.

The Lake Selling Hurdle which took palce at the meeting on Friday November 21st, 1986 was later to appear on the B.B.C's Question of Sport, 'what happened next slot'. Only Five Yards from the line rookie jockey Kevin Sims Fell off the 7-4 Favourite Taylors Renovation.

As owner Jeffrey Ross told Eamonn Gavigan of the Evening Post *"I've seen this happen to other horses, but like everything else you never think it will happen to you. But that's racing and you have never won until the jockey has weighed in".*

The story did not end there though. For it came to light that an uncle of Alex Whitting, who was also a racehorse trainer, put a curse on Nottingham racecourse that no member of his family would train a winner there. Subsequently Alex Whitting arranged for a priest to exorcise the spirit of his long departed uncle.

On the 30th October 1989 Lingfield became the first British Racecourse to hold an all-weather flat meeting. While two days later Southwell became the first to hold a National Hunt one. However if Messrs Ron and Richard Muddle had had their way, Nottingham would now be in their ownership as well as being an All-Weather Track.

After selling Lingfield for £7m they were able to make significant moves in an attempt to turn Colwick Park into the Ascot of the Midlands as Derek Thompson said at the time.

In December 1988 the Muddle's announced their £8.5 million intended package for Nottingham, of which the Levy Board were contributing £1m towards the costs. The majority of the money going on a brand new £5m grandstand.

Mr Richard Muddle said to the Evening Post of 16th December 1988 that:- *"The facilities are outdated for the modern public and are desperately in need of capital. Nottingham as a city offers* modern leisure opportunities although the racecourse, with declining attendance's cannot compete without heavy investment.

Attendance's are about the same as a good car boot sale. And they show a declining trend. This indicates the public do not find the present facilities particularly attractive. Generally racecourse attendance's are on the increase, especially at tracks where there has been considerable investment and improvement. Nottingham has varied and competitive leisure facilities and we find this an exciting challenge and look forward to repeating our past successes of Lingfield Park. This in no way criticises the present management who have only recently taken over under the chairmanship of Mr Player. Their board appear naturally cautious and we have therefore given assurances regarding the future of their position, that of existing staff, and legal guarantees regarding the future of Colwick Park as a racecourse. They have therefore left the decision in the hands of the Jockey Club, who say that any decision by them must be in the best interests of racing. Nottingham is centrally located between the three main racing centres of Lambourn in Berkshire, Newmarket and Malton in Yorkshire. The city is easily accessible by road and in an area of high population. The track also needs investment".

In reply Mr Peter Player, Chairman of the Nottingham Racecourse Company said:- "At present we have three very fine grass tracks - flat steeplechasing and hurdle. The course is renowned for being a level galloping track on which all types of horses have the fairest possible chance. This is proved by the number of good horses that have raced at Nottingham in recent years, such as Derby Winner Slip Anchor and Triple Crown Winner Oh So Sharp. For jumping enthusiasts, we have the famous City Trail Hurdle and past *winners include Comedy of Errors, who went on to win the Champion Hurdle twice. At present we can accommodate a huge field for all three types of racing, giving excellent betting opportunities. These figures will be significantly reduced if Mr Muddle's plans go ahead. It is his plan that jumping and flat racing should take place on the same grass course. This would be very detrimental to the going for the flat season, and leading trainers such as Henry Cecil and Michael Stoute would not be prepared to race potentially high class horses on cut up ground. Our attendance figures are increasing, some of our flat days have been up by as much as 30 per cent and this year we achieved some evenings with more than 4,000 people. We have queues of national and local firms wishing to sponsor races and entertain clients. We are completing a £175,000 40-room hostel for the often forgotten stable lads. There are plans to rebuild the weighing with private boxes above. Because the board is made up of mostly local people, we believe we have the interests of Nottingham racegoers at heart".*

While Councillor Mrs Betty Higgins, leader of the controlling Labour Party on the City Council, who then and still do, own the course said:- *I question whether Mr Muddle's plans are the best thing for Nottingham racecourse. I accept he has the money and is anxious to put it in. But I am concerned whether it is good for Nottingham to have this alongside the grass track. This will detract from the grass track which I understand is one of the best in the country. I fear there will be no jumping over hurdles on the grass track. Hurdling would be on the all-weather track and that is not popular".*

On December 20th, 1988 the City Council called a halt to the all weather proposition , when after the committee meeting they decided against allowing the use of some adjoining land.

Michaelozo who won the substitute St. Ledger 1989, gained his first career win in the one mile 50 yard Slip Anchor Stakes at Nottingham on Monday April 17th, 1989, when ridden by Paul Eddery to a ten length success. Starting at 13-2, he was the Cecil second string, as far as the punters were concerned for the Steve Cauthen ridden Belhommie started an evens favourite only to finish 4th of 5 runners. Michaelozo though after a variety of problems and a spell in France, is now a shadow of his former self.

If Michaelozo was one of the lesser Classic Winners to race at Nottingham, later that year racegoers saw a really great classic horse. For on Monday 4th September Salsabil won the six furlong Usher Maiden Stakes for two-year-olds fillies., in the hands of Willie Carson. The John Dunlop trained filly won by three lengths having started a 5-4 on favourite. Owned by Sheikh Hamden at Maktoum she went onto win three classics in 1990. After having won the 1,000 Guineas and the Oaks, Salsabil became the first filly for ninety years to win the Irish Derby.

During 1990 Salsabil was not the only Sheikh Hamden star Willie Carson was to ride. For the champion sprinter Dayjur trained by Major Dick Hern, opened his seasonal account in the six furlong Headingly Stakes for three-year-olds at Nottingham on May Day with an easy two length win. But not even his most ardent admirer that day could have forecast the roller coaster of successes he would have to endure.

For after winning Sandown's Temple Stakes, Royal Ascot's Stand Stakes, the Keeneland Nunthorpe Stakes at York, the Ladbroke Sprint Cup and the Prix De L'Abbaye on Arc day, came an extraordinary scene. One that rates on a par with Devon Loch's collapse in the Grand National of 1956. With the Breeder's Cup Sprint at Belmont Park his for the taking, Dayjur jumped a shadow when only twenty yards from the winning post.

In 1987 See You Then became the fourth and so far last horse to win three champion hurdles. Unfortunatly he did not have the best of legs, and when going for a record fourth he broke down in his Cheltenhem prep at Fontwell.

However after two years off it was decided by connections to bring him back. His return to the track being Nottinghams City Trial hurdle on February 17th, 1990 in which he was ridden by a local jockey Steve Smith-Eccles., The ending though was not a happy one, for as they say "they dont come back". He finished six of eight beaten a total of fifty two lengths behind the winner Royal Derbi.

At the time of writing the current Cheltenham Gold Cup Winner (1993), is considered to be a cut above the average. But then we seem to say that about most winner's of the race, as if we're looking for a spiritual reincarnation of Golden Miller or Arkle.

Jodami made his debut over obstacles on the 22nd January 1991 in Nottingham's Wilford Novices Hurdle over 2 miles. Even then he showed that staying power and guts would always be his strong point winning by 1 length in the hands of Patrick Farrell.

Chapter Fourteen

A New Beginning

On the 21st October 1990 Nottingham Racecourse unveiled it's plans to drag itself into the 20th century. The Evening Post of the following day carried a story which was headlined *"£1.3m bid to woo punters".*The plan was to rebuild the weighing room incorporating a new members stand, offices and private entertainment facilities. As Mr Peter Player said *"we view this development as the beginning of an exciting new era at Colwick Park Racecourse. I believe our new building will allow us to compete very effectively both in the corporate market and in attracting individual racegoers".*

The New Grandstand

His belief in the project was so strong that he went onto say *"I am determined Nottingham will be a success - or I shall resign, as being a total failure"*.

Dessie Infront Of The New Stand

As soon as the work started, the next momentous occasion was the burying of a time capsule. This was done directly in front of the Centenary Stand, by two of the greatest ambassadors the sport has ever known, in Peter Scudamore and Steve Cauthen. With the work on the stand , on schedule to replace the old weighing room which had benn in existence since the course opened in 1892.

The time capsule was lowered into place on the 23rd September 1991. Steve Cauthen was quoted in the following day's Evening Post:- *"Nottingham has always been a good racecourse and it's nice to see they are building this new stand. It's* definitely good for racing to have better facilities for the public and jockeys. It can only encourage more people to enjoy the sport".

While Tom Hiscock the then commercial manager said:- "It will give us a very high quality facility that will hopefully last longer than the next 100 years. We want to encourage people to get back into the habit of racing. This year we've had good crowds. We've been quite pleased because many courses have seen crowds fall because of the recession".

Tom James a bookmaker of 30 years experience told me "that the Nottingham Stewards Cup is one of the hardest races for bookies to book on, as ones drawn on the stands side which are well backed usually win". He also said "In over 30 years of betting he has never made it pay at Nottingham, as course is so fair especially for two-year-olds".

The last part explains the reasoning behind why so many leading flat trainers send the top two-year-olds to Nottingham for their racecourse debut.

One final tale told me by Tom James goes back to the Monday of October 21st 1991 for the 6 furlong Keyworth H'cap. In which Maurice Camacho's Twilight Falls opened at 12-1. Three men stood close to Tom James, Leslie Steele & W.Boden and at a given moment they took all the available prices down to 6-1. The end result being he ran out an easy 1 a half length winner in the hands of John Lowe. The bookie's words were "that one made him cough".

As the work was moving steadily along the course received a visit on 22nd October 1991, by the senior steward of the Jockey Club Lord Hartington. Whom to say the least was highly impressed for, as he said:- *"I'ts the first time I've been here since the stands were re-built. But now they are up and nearly ready it's very exciting. Nottingham has got an exceptionally enthusiastic and aggressive management team".*

The last statement referred to Peter Player as Chairman, Major Charles Moore as Clerk of the Course, the late John Parrett as executive director, Sheila Payne as company secretary and Tom Hiscocks as commercial manager.

On that same day a meagre 819 paid to go through the turnstiles, but everyone concerned were not taking matters lightly. For as Charles Moore said in the following Day's Evening Post *"I am afraid we've become pretty down trodden. But we live on the edge of a pretty rich town. And we just need to make people aware of racing and how much fun it is".*

While Peter Player stated *"Newmarket and Windsor evening fixtures have become something of a cult and I see 9,000 at a Pontefract meeting. We've just got to sell ourselves and make it inviting for husbands and wives to come to Nottingham".*

As like most racecourses Nottingham are increasingly looking towards their non racing days, so as to maximise their annual income. For instance as Tom Hiscocks said *"We are member of a body called Conference Nottingham. They place a lot of international and nation-wide conferences in the city. We are in a position to take*

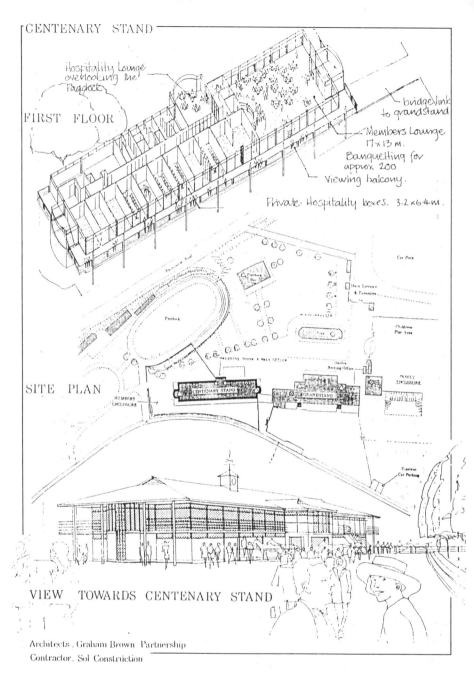

CENTENARY STAND

Hospitality Lounge
overlooking the
Paddock

FIRST FLOOR

bridge link
to grandstand

Members Lounge
17 x 13 m.

Banquetting for
approx. 200

Viewing balcony.

Private Hospitality boxes. 3.2 x 6.4 m.

SITE PLAN

MEMBERS
ENCLOSURE

Paddock

Car Park

Main Entrance
& Turnstiles

Children's
Play Area

FAMILY
ENCLOSURE

VIEW TOWARDS CENTENARY STAND

Architects. Graham Brown Partnership
Contractor. Sol Construction

The New Colwick Site Plan

a lot of business. We've got a central conference hall for 150 to 200 people, with other room for satellite meetings and discussion groups".

On the racing side he went onto say:- "We are trying to create a mass awareness of the sport in Nottingham. When we had a ladies night, there was a 42% bigger crowd than the previous year, and 28% were first time racegoers".

While a number of councils have been off loading their interests in racecourses because of Government legislation. Nottingham though took the opposite view. This course of action is only now reaping dividends, something that was echoed by Lord Hartington, for as he told the Evening Post:- "A lot of local authorities are not keen on having a racecourse. But the Nottingham civil authorities are very enthusiastic and consider it to be part of the amenities of their city. Peter Player is very energetic and very go-ahead. Nick Forman Hardy is a local businessman who regards it as an exciting challenge and also sees it as part of the amenities of Nottingham".

The last named apart from being on the board of the racecourse committee, is also owner of the Nottingham Evening Post.

Later on Lord Hartington went onto give a big vote to Nottingham's decision to employ a commercial manager. Incidentally they became one of the first racecourses in the country to have one, when Tom Hiscocks took up the post in December 1990. However he has since left.

As the Senior Steward stated:- *"For a comparatively small racecourse like Nottingham to take the brave step of employing a full-time commercial manager, is a very good example of how racing can look after itself. It's all part of what the Home Affairs Committee and Sir John Sparrow, the Chairman of the Levy Board want to see. That is to extract as much commercial value on non racing days. It's not easy selling corporate hospitality boxes at the moment. But when the upturn in the economy comes, Nottingham will be in a good position to take advantage."*

Various personalities I've talked to spoke highly of Colwick Park. For instance leading trainer Jack Berry said *"The new image, weighing room coupled with the better cards is a vast improvement"*. While Peter Scudamore described it *"as a good course to ride on"*. Peter Easterby simply described *"it as a good course and a big improvement of late"*.

February 15th 1992 apart from being the highlight of their centenary year, it was also the dawning of a new era. The racing was of the highest class.

One of the leading trials for the Champion Hurdle, is Nottingham's City Trial Hurdle Ltd Handicap a limited handicap over two miles.

For the City Trial Hurdle he carried bottom weight of 10stone 7lbs and in retrospect he was a handicap certainty. He started a well backed 11-10 on favourite, even though he was 9lbs out of the handicap. Taking the lead going to the last hurdle, he ran out an easy 3 a half length winner, ridden yet again by Graham McCourt. The next stop for Royal Gait was the Champion Hurdle which he won in impressive style.

Sharing top billing with the City Trial Hurdle, was the Nottinghamshire Novices Chase over two miles. A race that went to the 13-8 joint favourite Deep Sensation, who went onto win the Queen Mother Two Mile Champion Chase at the Cheltenham Festival a year later.

The main attraction that day for the majority of people was Desert Orchid. This was his first appearance since retirement. For he was there to open the new members stand and weighing room, or rather Mrs Midge Burridge one of the joint owners of Desert Orchid did. As it was she who unveiled the plaque that marked the opening of the complex.

The management were more than pleased with the turnout and they felt it was the start of better things. For as Peter Player told the Evening Post of February 17th 1992:-

"There was a marvellous atmosphere, something that has been missing from Nottingham for a long time. This is just the first step in our long-term plans and we hope we can make every day at Colwick Park like Saturday. We are on our way now. This was just the start of our improvements and upgrading for Nottingham and when we are finished it will be known as racing's Mecca of the Midland's. We are getting a better standard of horse here now and owners and trainers have been complimentary about our improvement both on the track and on the facilities side. Obviously we have a lot of people to thank for our present position and I was

delighted how everything went according to plan on Saturday. We have had very little money to play with over the years and it is due to a lot of hard work by the board and our staff that we have resurrected Nottingham. We are trying to get an atmosphere back and I feel we are almost there. It's nice when people actually congratulate you on what you have done. At least you know they are taking notice. I am not, easily satisfied. And with the help of the people of Nottingham we will create a racing and leisure area that we will all be proud to call our own, where the high standards of service and value for money will be the watchwords".

So here's to the next 100 years of racing at Colwick Park.

*Aerial View Of Colwick Park: c1960: The One Mile Straight
No Longer Exists.*

Page 191

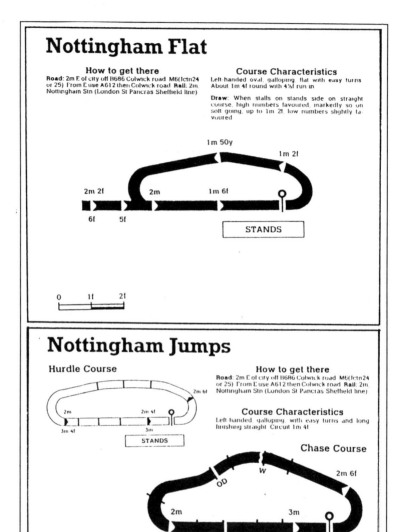

Nottingham Flat

How to get there
Road: 2m E of city off B686 Colwick road. M6(Jctn24 or 25) From E use A612 then Colwick road. **Rail:** 2m, Nottingham Stn (London St Pancras Sheffield line)

Course Characteristics
Left-handed oval, galloping, flat with easy turns About 1m 4f round with 4½f run in

Draw: When stalls on stands side on straight course, high numbers favoured, markedly so on soft going, up to 1m 2f, low numbers slightly favoured

1m 50y
1m 2f
2m 2f
2m
1m 6f
6f   5f

STANDS

0   1f   2f

Nottingham Jumps

Hurdle Course

How to get there
Road: 2m E of city off B686 Colwick road. M6(Jctn24 or 25) From E use A612 then Colwick road. **Rail:** 2m, Nottingham Stn (London St Pancras Sheffield line)

Course Characteristics
Left-handed, galloping, with easy turns and long finishing straight. Circuit 1m 4f

2m 6f
2m   2m 4f
3m 4f   3m
STANDS

Chase Course

W
OD
2m 6f
2m   3m
3m 4f   OD
STANDS

0   1f   2f

The Flat And The Jump Courses

Index

Organza	127	Puergere	74
Oxo	99	Purefoy, Captian H.R.	75
Paget, Dorothy	34,35,75,114	Queen Imaal	99
	118,119,122,123	Queen Mother	164
	127,138,139,141	R.A.F. Swinderby	12,148
Palermo	136,137	Railway	150
Pamona	10,24	Rating, Tom	158
Pampas Grass	51	Ravenspur	72
Paradise Club	141	Red Rum	78,114,154,158
Parella	106	Red, Carrie	48
Parfrement, Georges	93,95,98,99	Reeves, Herbert	103
Parrett, John	185	Regal	46
Payne, William	98,99,112	Reine Des Pres	70
Payne, J.	112	Resolved	152
Payne, Sheila	185	Reugny	46
Paynter, Colonel G.	109	Rhodes, J.	101
Perryman, Dick	127	Rhodes, A.	101
Persimmon	74	Rich Gift	107
Peter	46	Richards, Sir Gordon	11,118,115,119
Phychic Bid	139		123
Piggott, Lester	13,16,69,155	Richards, Lynda	164,124,148
	161,162,163	Richards, Cliff	130
	164,172	Richardson, Charles	84
Piggott, Keith	107	Rickaby, Fred	69,133
Piggott, Ernie	78,95,109	Rickman, John	70
Pinza	124	Rimell Mercy	159
Player, Mr Peter	160,164,177	Rimell, Fred	131,136,139
	182,185,187	Robinson, Peter	152
	189,146	Robinson. Sir John	89
Pledge, Mr W.	101	Robinsons, Mr C.J.	73
Poacher	76	Rodgers, Charlie	138
Portland, Duke Of	29,69,148	Roi Hero	103,104,107
Prescott, Sir Mark	144	Roi Herode	104
Pretty Boy	31	Roker	104
Prince Hampton	74	Roman	96
Prince Herod	103	Roman Hackle	141
Prince Bismark	71	Romeo	74
Provider	90	Ross, Jeffrey	176
Psiduim	117	Rosslare	98

Credits For Illustrations